HEARTLAND PORTRAIT

FREE RIVER PRESS
FOLK LITERATURE SERIES

Robert Wolf, General Editor

HEARTLAND PORTRAIT
Stories and Essays of Rural Life

Selected and Edited
by
Robert Wolf

Illustrations by Bonnie Koloc

FREE RIVER PRESS

ISBN#1-878781-17-0
© Copyright 1995
by Free River Press

Heartland Portrait contains material from

Voices from the Land © Copyright 1992
    by Free River Press
Simple Times © Copyright 1993
    by Free River Press
More Voices from the Land © Copyright 1994
    by Free River Press
Clermont, Iowa © Copyright 1994
    by Free River Press and
    Clermont Community Club

Acknowledgements
The publisher is grateful to the following authors for permission
to reprint passages from copyrighted material:

Delores Martin for permission to reprint "The Flood"
    from *Independence, Iowa,* © Copyright 1994 by
    Connie's Hallmark and White Funeral Home
Hannah Chesmore for permission to reprint "$4.95"
    from *Independence, Iowa,* © Copyright 1994 by
    Connie's Hallmark and White Funeral Home

Contents

INTRODUCTION

This book grew out of three years of work in rural Iowa, three years of running writing workshops for farm families and residents of rural towns. Several books emerged from these workshops, the first of which, *Voices from the Land,* received national attention, thanks to features on National Public Radio's "Morning Edition" and an Associated Press story that ran in almost every major daily in the country. From the sales and letters that the writers and I received from people across America, I became convinced that there was a great hunger in this land for things rural. Even a year or so after the appearance of that first book, I continued to receive letters and phone calls from urbanites responding to stories on it.

Buoyed in part, I suppose, by this response, we continued for a second year, and kept producing books. *Simple Times,* the second in the series, was written by our oldest member, the now 86-year-old Clara Leppert, and recounts her life from 1909 to roughly 1950.

Then came *More Voices from the Land,* another anthology by the authors of *Voices from the Land,* which focused more on the ongoing farm crisis. During the same period I began running workshops in northeast Iowa towns, whose purpose was to produce self-portraits of those towns. Stories from two of those books, *Independence, Iowa,* and *Clermont, Iowa,* are included in this volume.

But *Heartland Portrait* is far more than an account of northeast Iowa, for what happens here is happening everywhere in rural America, a fact that cannot be overemphasized. Even those who do not live in rural America know that rural towns have a disproportionately high population of the elderly, that the family farm is fast disappearing, that rural America lacks an industrial base, that poverty is widespread.

There is more reason than nostalgia for urbanites to read this book. There is a deep interconnection between the country and the city, deeper than the connection of food producer to consumer, and it has to do with quantitative methodologies and the growth of centralized power and collectives that govern all our lives. The growth of production efficient methods (which put small farmers out of business) and powerful corporations (which monopolize farm profits) and the state and national legislatures (which tell us, wisely or not, how to use our land) have left many rural Americans poor and powerless. Wealth, concentrated in the cities, continues flowing to the cities, and there is nothing that rural Americans have been able to do about it. It is that powerlessness in the face of the great collectives that has led so many rural Americans to see the federal government as their oppressor.

2

2.

This book is part of the Free River Press folk literature series, which began in Nashville, Tennessee, with a writing workshop for homeless men and women. From the homeless project, out of which eventually came six books, emerged a larger vision. After a year and a half spent on the homeless project I decided to create a fuller record of American life.

The impulse to document American life goes back to my very early interest in the writers and painters of the American scene. In high school I was enthralled by the visions of America that I read in the poems of Langston Hughes and Carl Sandburg, in the novels and stories of John Dos Passos, Jack Kerouac, and William Saroyan, and saw in the paintings and murals of Diego Rivera and Thomas Hart Benton, Grant Wood and John Stuart Curry.

Between all of these sources I developed a hunger for things distinctly American, and a desire to search them out. I wanted to work every job in the country and to live in every town. I wanted endless conversations with characters of all types.

For years I hitchhiked and rode freights across country and lived in various towns and cities, fulfilling part of my dream to live and work among all manner of men and women, in all parts of the country. But instead of working all the jobs, I now get others to document their lives for me. And that is how this book came about, this compilation of smaller books from the Free River Press Heartland Series, which itself is merely part of a larger projected series documenting American life in the second half of the twentieth century, written mostly by people without literary ambition.

3.

Heartland Portrait describes, sometimes explicitly and sometimes indirectly, the impact of technology on farming practices, the land, and community. In the course of my work in Iowa I have found that what is true for rural Iowa is true for the rest of rural America. Those of us who live in the countryside, whether in Ohio, Kentucky, Tennessee, Mississippi, Iowa, Kansas, or in any of a dozen other states, share the same problems. *Heartland Portrait* describes rural problems in the words of rural residents, but it also describes possible solutions.

I spent several year contemplating how one could go about rebuilding regional economies which had once flourished in the United States, and the last section of this book tells how I think the rebuilding might proceed, from the redirection of the individual to the rebuilding of towns and finally to the coalescence of area towns into regional cities, and regional cities into a larger regional economy.

My conversations with people here on the need for a self-sufficient regional economy have awakened me to the divisions within and between rural towns, divisions perhaps too deep ever to repair. Fragmentation, I have often thought, is the driving force of our time, far more powerful than any integrating force. Thus it often seems that any integrating ideas that might emerge, no matter whose, will not be acted on. There is envy here, as elsewhere, and rural towns, like urban areas, may be far too divided ever to unite. Perhaps, after further dissolution, after a time of many years when our local, state, and federal governments will have been reduced to a pro forma existence, then perhaps communities will emerge.

4.

The farm books grew out of a writing workshop that first met in the farmhouse of Bill and Esther Welsh, organic farmers and friends of my wife and I. In fact, it was Bill and Esther who first helped me recruit and organize the workshop. Bruce Carlson, the Lansing dentist, had told me about them. I had told Bruce that I wanted to start a farm writing workshop, and he suggested that I contact Bill, an organic farmer very much involved in community issues.

A few months later, the local paper announced that the Welsh Family Organic Farm was hosting a tour of their operation, and I realized that this was my opportunity to begin recruiting. As we were escorted around the buildings I met another of my neighbors, Bob Leppert, who was the first in our area to adopt organic farming methods. I talked to Bob about a workshop as we trudged about, explaining that the book would offer farmers the opportunity to say to the public what they wanted about the ongoing farm crisis. I explained the success we'd had getting national attention for the homeless books, and Bob was interested. We made a date to meet at his home a few nights later.

The same day, after the tour, we all sat inside the Welsh's garage on folding chairs, and socialized. I talked to Bill Welsh, and to Greg, his eldest son, who at once realized that the book represented an opportunity to present so much of rural life, including the emerging organic revolution. I told the Welshes I would be back in touch with them.

A few nights later I spent three to four hours talking with Bob Leppert until midnight, an intense conversation I can recall to this day: the kind of passionate conversation young college students generally have, full of conviction and ranging over many subjects. It was Bob's passion and conviction, and above all his deep integrity, that I remember to this day.

Shortly after that Bob and I visited the Welshes, drawing up a list of names of possible participants. Three months later, when we finally met on a Monday night around the Welshes twelve-foot-long dining table, there were seven of us, three farming couples—Bill and Esther Welsh, Bob and Barb Leppert, Danny and Frances Cole, and myself. Danny dropped out but Clara Leppert, Bob's mother, Bruce Carlson, the Lansing dentist, and Greg Welsh joined us. Others came by briefly, among them Dorothy and Richard Sandry.

We began meeting shortly before Christmas 1991, and met every Monday after evening chores, rotating from one farmhouse to another, until spring planting. For me it provided community; perhaps for the others too. Certainly they anticipated each week's meeting, not only for the writing and the reading and the reactions they got to their work, but for the socializing afterwards, when the hosts would bring out tea and coffee, sandwich makings or desserts. They called it lunch.

Over food and coffee we would discuss the loss of community, the decline of the national economy, the problems of the family farm, and ways to counteract the dissolution we saw everywhere. And I would think to myself, "If only some of my city friends could hear these conversations!" Without being there, they would find it hard to believe the level of sophistication. Besides, some of my urban friends had the most absurd views of rural life, considering it an aberration and their own frantic existence, sensible.

Most of us had separate agendas for the project. I had told the farmers that once each of them had finished a piece that we would give public readings with discussion afterwards in which they would be able to engage urban audiences, and that those discussions would be the heart of the project.

I anticipated that my neighbors would impress urban audiences, and they did. After their reading in La Crosse, Wisconsin, a college professor remarked, "I thought people like that died out forty years ago!" He was impressed with their dignity and integrity.

I am extremely fortunate to live among them. Having resided in ten states, among all sorts and conditions of people, I have seldom met their like. They live the agrarian ideal that Jefferson wanted for this country: they are the virtuous citizens that he dreamed would fill the continent.

Their writings are record of a community that once existed here, of the growing costs and instability of farming, of the love of the land. It is a document that will endure.

ROBERT WOLF

Part I:
SIMPLE TIMES

Foreword

Writing that transmits culture passes on information, technical or otherwise. In the Middle Ages this information was frequently transmitted under the guise of a good story, but nowadays we often find a split between entertainment and information. There is seldom that split for folk writers, who are concerned with passing on the stuff of their lives: local history, customs, thoughts, daily relations. And they do so in a matter-of-fact way. Their writing is of a piece with their lives.

Clara Leppert's writing is a reflection of Clara, and exemplifies the best qualities of good folk writing: it is direct, plain, and unpretentious. When she read one of her pieces for a National Public Radio story, people called from across the country, wanting to know how they could get the book that contained the story "Wolves."

Clara's voice, its intonation and wonderful quavering sweetness, itself evokes qualities of long ago. No wonder, for Clara—unworldly, living and growing up in a corner of northeastern Iowa—has in effect remained untouched by the corruption of a world increasingly urbanized, increasingly mechanized, increasingly depersonalized.

Only after living in northeastern Iowa for one year could I begin to understand how rootedness in place, without heavy dependence on rapid transportation, provided the nurturing for community. The rootedness of small towns and rural populations in the last century was what gave many American communities their distinct qualities. For the farm families, who usually traveled to town no more than once a week, this engendered an unworldliness, a self-reliance, and, at the same time, an understanding of the need for community.

When the present crop of farmers passes away, with them will go their way of life and their simplicity, directness, and honesty. For the urban dweller, so often armored with cynicism, this seems quaint, unbelievable, hardly enviable. But the problem is that once these farmers go, we have only written records to show us how people once behaved in community. And the cynics are likely to deny that such community ever existed, thus making it ever more difficult to recapture.

But Clara's book, I believe, will remain as a record of what rural life was once like, and a reminder of how it might be rebuilt. Not so much with technical know-how as with benevolence and the qualities which make a man or woman a full human being. It has been a delight knowing this wonderful eighty-six-year-old neighbor.

ROBERT WOLF

Prologue

I was born May 3, 1909. As I grew up, I loved to climb trees. I would sit on a branch close to the top and not hold on to anything. It would scare my younger sisters.

I loved to ride horses. I wanted them to be spirited so they would be speedy.

I liked the peppy popular music.

It was fun to go to my dad's woods, watch the creek as it rippled, and listen as it sang a song. We picked May flowers, violets, blood root, and Dutchman Breeches.

Now, I am older. I don't even care to climb a ladder, and would be scared to get on a horse.

I love soft music, especially waltzes.

It is a joy to send cards to relatives and friends who have a special day.

I love to go to church and sing and pray with the others. If I am awake at night I pray. Someone said, "If you can't sleep at night, don't count sheep, talk to the Shepherd."

I am Clara

I am Clara, the middle daughter. I was born on a sunny, warm spring day, May 3, 1909 at the home of my parents, Adolph Siekmeier and Carolena (Lena) Nagel. Uncle Jake Siekmeier wrote in the *North Fork*, a local paper, "After a long, dreary, cold winter, baby Siekmeier brings spring." My older sisters are Mary, Anna, and Lydia, the younger are Esther, Ruth, and Dorothy.

Mother said Dad wanted me to be named Clara, because it was a good Danish name, but he couldn't say it very well. He called me Clarie. My younger sisters called me La La or Da Da.

I am glad to have grown up in a family where we were taught to love the Lord and to go to Sunday school and church. One of the first things I remember from my childhood is family devotions. After we ate breakfast, Dad read a chapter out of the Bible, and we all knelt by our chairs while he prayed. Again in the evening, before we went to bed, he read another chapter from the Bible.

We usually wore white dresses to church. We put large bows in our braided hair and wore hats and gloves. It was very important to have a new hat and dress for Easter and new clothes for Christmas services. Our skirts had lace and tucks and were starched. Unless our dresses were plenty heavy, we had to wear two skirts. Even though we usually had braids, our hair would get tangled, and we would yell when our older sisters combed our hair.

Mother usually shaved Dad Sunday mornings. If he got shaved in town she would reprimand him saying, "Why did you get shaved in town? You know I would have shaved you." If he didn't get shaved in town, she'd ask, "Why didn't you get shaved in town? Now I have to shave you."

We drove to church with horses and buggy or sled. Dad had quincy quite a lot in the winter time. He finally had to have his tonsils out. If he couldn't go to church, Mother would drive. Some of the winters we had a lot of snow. For two miles we would have to go up high banks or in people's fields, and sometimes the sled would tip over. We'd have to pick up the straw and blankets and get back in. When the next two miles were graveled, the snow scraping off the sled made a gritty noise, but it didn't seem hard for the horses to pull. They were always well fed and well taken care of. When we got to church we had to tie the horses in the hitching yard and put blankets on them to keep them from getting chilled. Every Sunday, Mrs. Sherman would brush a little dust or horse hair from Mother's dark coat. The two families were always very good friends.

Years later, in 1918, Dad bought a one-passenger Buick. It had two jump seats. We had a really full load sometimes, but it would still move in mud up to the hubcaps. We'd have to get on our knees to put on the chains and hang side curtains. Side curtains fit on the side windows where modern cars have glass. On our way to church Dad would say, "Don't drive quite so fast," and Mother would say, "Drive a little faster or we're going to be late."

Farming a Long Time Ago

As I was growing up, farming was a family affair. Each person had a job. Dad always fed the pigs, but the women took care of the chickens and got the cows from the pasture. Dad planted the corn and sowed the oats. All of the farm work was done with horses. We girls helped with putting up hay, shocking grain, and husking corn. Mother would see to it that the younger ones brought us lunch. When each of us girls was about eight, we were old enough to milk a cow.

Mother took care of the big gas engine that turned the separator. I don't know how many times she fixed it. The milk was given to the pigs, and the cream hauler came for the cream that had been put in ten gallon cans. The hauler put these cans in his truck.

In the fall when the grain was ripe we girls shocked the grain, putting six bundles together, and one on top to keep the rain off. Barley bundles scratched our arms and made us itch. Later when the corn was ripe, we would husk it, two rows at a time. The horses would follow the rows and stop and go as we told them.

Putting up hay was a big job. Mother mowed the hay, and also ran the side deliver, a machine that put the hay in windrows. When the hay was dry, one of us girls would drive the horses on the hay rack, pulling the hay loader, which was a tall machine with rollers that rolled the hay onto the rack. Dad would distribute the hay evenly on the rack.

When we unloaded the hay, mother stuck the fork, which had two sharp prongs, into the hay. Then she'd push a lever that would hold the hay. The hay fork had a rope on it and at the other end of the barn you had two horses that would pull the fork and hay up high into the barn.

One of us girls would drive the team to the other side of the barn, pulling up the hay fork. Dad would yell "whoa" when the fork of hay was where he wanted it in the hay mow (the storage area), and mother would trip the fork. One time she didn't think and tied the rope to the hay rack. It raised quite high in the air before the horses could be stopped.

We had about three hundred chickens each year. It was a lot of work with the hens, who sometimes wouldn't set on their fifteen eggs, and we would cover the eggs with a box for awhile. We had to catch the hens, who sometimes pecked us, and put them in their little houses, then catch the fluffy little chickens when it rained. Mother had an incubator, and we turned all the eggs twice a day, I think, but it seemed that so many eggs didn't hatch.

We were all glad to do what we could to help. We loved each other and our faithful horses, and we loved our life on the farm.

Childhood Games

We liked to play horse, especially after a rain, as it was fun splashing in the mud. I was usually the horse driven by my younger sisters. We stuffed our dresses in our panties and Dad would say, "You are my little pants boys." I liked to hear him say that. I ate gooseberries, pretending it was oats. They were awfully sour, but it was fun, being that it bothered my sisters' ears.

We loved to walk to the woods. Mary had cleaned leaves away from a damp spot on the bluff. There was a little spring, we always called it "Mary's Little Spring." Sometimes we found pretty berries on the weeds to make our mud pies pretty. Dad never told anyone where an Indian grave was, he was afraid someone would dig it up, but we always looked for it.

We girls played a lot in the attic with our dolls, there were steps from the bathroom into the attic. We tenderly cared for our dolls and sewed for them, but their heads were so porcelain and so breakable. They were beautiful and had eyes that would go to sleep.

I Wasn't Always Good

I wasn't always good. I don't know if anyone knew I teased the huge turkey gobbler. I would stand on the safe side of the lawn fence, point my finger at him and say, "Gobble, gobble, gobble." He would get very angry and got so he would fly at us when we went in the big yard. Mother finally decided he had better be put in the big roasting pan.

I also teased Lydia's little terrier dog, pointing at her and saying, "Bow wow." One day I didn't get my left forefinger back in time and she took a piece of flesh out of it. I still have the scar.

One day I was asked to take the hammer back to the separator house. I thought, instead of carrying it there, it would be much more fun to drive by in the little wagon and throw it in. I had good speed on the little wagon and threw in the hammer as I had planned, but I didn't know anyone was in the building. I hit Anna smack on the head. She didn't scold me much, but she had a big lump on her head, of course, and I felt real sorry, but being sorry didn't help the lump.

One day Uncle Fred and Aunt Mary left their Ford car in Dad's machine shed, while they went away for a couple of days with Mother and Dad. Lydia and I didn't know how to run a car, but thought it would be great fun to try. One of us steered and the other gave a push and suddenly the Ford was down in the yard. We didn't know how to get the car started, but kept trying until we had it humming and sputtering and safely back in the shed again.

Family

We girls didn't do much quarrelling. It didn't pay to get Mother "riled up" and "after us", and if Dad heard us not talking very nice to each other he'd say, "Girls, don't rouse one another's tempers." I was too little to remember when he had a bad temper, but I remember Mother's temper very well. She spanked or whipped me many times. Sometimes I knew I had been naughty. Other times I didn't know what I had done wrong. One time I was standing by the range and she suddenly kept hitting me with a nice big pancake turner until it broke it two. I didn't feel sorry about the pancake turner, but my rear didn't feel so good for a long time. I never knew why I was whipped.

I was almost ten when Dorothy was born, but didn't know Mother was expecting a baby. Mother didn't seem well and didn't have loving patience with the new baby. Many evenings I walked around and around the house with Dorothy to get her to sleep. I liked to do it.

We weren't a huggy, kissy family, but we knew our parents loved us. I never remember sitting on either Dad or Mother's lap, but it was only once I saw Dad spank any of us.

Dad

Dad said, "Be thankful to have both jam and butter on your bread, many folks would be glad to have just bread." It got on his nerves when we "scratched" butter on our crackers, as he called it. He also didn't like it when we cut the bread thin. He had trouble with pronunciation, as I do yet. After learning the Danish language, and the German and English languages after coming to this country, some words were hard for him to say. He would tell us, "You cut the bread so tin, tin as a piece of paper," so we would try to do better the next time.

Dad loved bananas, they didn't have them in Denmark. When his family came to this country and were in Chicago on the way here, he was eating the whole banana when someone told him to take the peel off. He often bought bananas when he went to town, also chocolate stars and what he called little chocolate hills.

He didn't always go with us places, he visited people and talked about religion. He had a great knowledge of the Bible. Landsgards and others said they asked him to talk about the Bible to them. Landsgards, being Norwegian, could understand his Dane.

During his prime years, Dad was very strong. I was told he could bend a horseshoe straight, lift a barrel of salt, also lift the end of a threshing machine. At one time he carried a mule who wouldn't drink to the tank.

He said when he couldn't sleep, he was on his knees praying that all of us would go to Heaven.

We Loved Aunt Mary and Uncle Fred

We all loved Aunt Mary and Uncle Fred and were always glad when they came to see us. Aunt Mary was Mother's sister and Uncle Fred was Dad's brother. They didn't have any children, so they gave us much affection. I sat by Aunt Mary, knowing she would soon open up her purse and give me a cough drop. It took the place of candy. They were delicious. She would tell the story about "The Goat and the Seven Little Kids." I thought it was a terrible ghost story, but the next time she came, I would ask her to tell it again. One night when Aunt Mary stayed over she came to Mother's room in the middle of the night where us younger ones slept, knelt by Mother's bed and said, "Lena, my heart, my heart. I'm dying." It surely scared me, but Mother got out of bed and gave her something to comfort her. She seemed all right the next day.

When Aunt Mary and Uncle Fred came to see us they would leave as soon as they had eaten dinner because Uncle Fred was afraid a storm would come up. One day Dad said, "Can't you stay a little longer? There isn't a cloud in the sky." The sky was as beautiful clear and blue as a jewel. Uncle Fred said, "No, the wind might blow up a storm and it might rain." Aunt Mary and Uncle Fred never had a lot of money, but she bought each of my sisters and me a ring for our confirmations. Mine is a yellow sapphire. It will always be very special.

The McCabe's

I helped out at five or six places. It was a very hard thing for me to do, but the folks felt it was the only Christian thing to do. I helped Cora McCabe with cleaning and at threshing. It wasn't easy to keep an even temperature with the ranges, sometimes the pie burned, but she would calmly say, "Just snag off a little bit of the black." Wages weren't big, but I was proud walking home with a quarter in my pocket.

We and the McCabes were always very good friends. We went to the Catholic church for their children's first communion and confirmation. As we went up the steps, the friendly people would say, "You can sit in our pew." It seems to me there must have been fifty or sixty young children receiving their first communion. The girls were all dressed with white veils and dresses.

Peddlers

We had a peddler who came every month or two for years. He came in the evening so he could stay overnight. We had to wait until morning to see what he had in his big leather-like bag. He always gave mother coffee beans to grind to prove he had good coffee. He had dress fabric and a lot of things. He gave us kids little trinkets.

We all felt bad when Lydia had blood poisoning in her arm. A man came selling Watkins or something (they drove horses yet), and he wanted to prove his salve was good. We put salve on a sore on her arm, and we felt that caused the poisoning. Dr. Huecker came every day for fourteen days, and lanced it in five places. She had a lot of pain. When she would cry we were told to go down the lane a ways. Her arm was very stiff. Mother had a little outfit with rubber wheels, she colled her arm every night. Her arm never got so she could bend it like her right arm. We were glad she got along as well as she did.

Christmas

Christmas was always a big event. We looked forward to the Christmas Eve program at church, to our sacks of nuts and, maybe, to an apple and orange. Those who could, paid for the sacks. We would get a gift from our Sunday school teacher. It was good to hear the people sing, "Der Christbaum ist der Schonste Baum" as the candles were lit. In English it was "The Christmas tree is the fairest tree." Candles were in little metal holders. Men stood with a wet mop to put a little fire out if it started.

The program was very special. Dad didn't go, but he would stay up to put the horses in the barn. Mother drove the horses' sled. There were probably deep snow drifts for two miles. We had to go on the banks of the road and through some fields, and then for two miles on gravel. The sled runners made lots of noise and we felt sorry for the horses. When we got to town, people were driving around the streets, the bells on the horses' harness making such beautiful Christmas music.

Town

     I often drove Nellie or Daisy, our horses, to help drive cattle to town to sell. These were war times. We didn't have much white flour. We could only buy fifty pounds worth of sugar at a time. After we got to town Dad gave each of us a dollar. We decided right away to get fifty cents worth of sugar each to help out on Mother's baking. We still had fifty cents left. It said on the window of the Red Geranium cafe: banana splits fifty cents. We walked by many times looking at the pretty picture of the banana split. It looked so good, and we had never had one, but fifty cents was a lot of money. We finally decided to spend it and slowly ate our banana split. Beside the banana there were three kinds of ice cream and lots of syrup and a red cherry on each dip of ice cream. We always remember that special event.

     One day Ruth and I went to town to take food to Esther, who was rooming there. We had the cutter which tipped easily. Unexpectedly, the cutter runners followed the railroad track instead of crossing it and tipped over and the horses ran away. We had to stop when one was on each side of a telephone pole. Daisy was hurt quite badly and was never quite as good any more. Dad felt awfully bad. I did too. He said, "It's too late for this time, watch out for the next."

     One day we had a phone call. The horse we had loaned Uncle Fred was in town, and he was through with her. I was to get her, tying her behind the buggy. She looked pretty old and feeble, but I tied her behind the buggy and started for home. I went on the road past Aunt Ida's and Uncle Herman's to avoid going past the train. Uncle Herman was on the porch. He said, "You'll never get that horse home alive Clara," but I did. It was a slow trip. The horses walked all the way, but I did get home all right.

School and Town

     I was a freshman when Anna and Lydia were seniors. For the first time I didn't have to wear long underwear. My legs felt so nice and slender, I didn't care if they did get cold.

     I was tall, but thin. A few people asked me if I was teaching school. Alice and Helen McCabe would ask, "How tall are you Clara? You are about as tall as a tree, aren't you?"

     We drove Kate, a white horse, or a team of horses to school. When it got real cold we stayed at Uncle Fred Nagel's apartment over a tavern. In the evening Uncle Fred would walk back and forth, memorizing his Masonic lecture. We girls all slept in one bed. We nailed fabric to a folding screen to have privacy when Uncle Fred or his son, Ray, walked by. The manager of the tavern downstairs asked Uncle Fred if we were cracking nuts because we were making so much noise hammering the covering on the frame. When Ray came home late and was sick, we would be scared and didn't sleep much those nights.

When we walked on the sidewalks, the city children called us hayseeds and other names. We didn't say anything, but it hurt. When it came to graduation, it was a hayseed who was valedictorian.

My second year in high school I rode Nellie or walked the four miles if Dad needed her in the field. I left her in a livery stable, the caretaker unsaddled and saddled her for me. After school I always had to wait until the train went by for Nellie to stop switching and snorting, as she was terribly afraid of it.

In the winter, I boarded with Mrs. Snitker right across from what we called Beeman (West) town. She didn't want to use too much electricity, so I had a kerosene lamp in my bedroom, but instead of studying, I read Zane Grey's books.

The third year I again rode Nellie or walked. The man at the livery stable seemed so nice and he had a little hut with a pot belly stove, where I could get my knickers off while he took care of Nellie. I stuffed my skirt into the knickers. Mother made them for us, they were like slacks, only they had a cuff just below the knee.

I stayed home a year after high school. I was only seventeen and too young to teach. Some of the days were very long, and I would look and look out of the window to see if my younger sisters were coming home from school.

Teaching

After I was through with high school I visited a pen pal I had for five years in Muscatine, Martha Freyermuth. She wanted me to come there and work in a canning factory with her, which I planned to do, until I was offered the chance to teach.

One day I was talking to a family friend, Ralph Leppert, in Waukon, and a man came and talked too. He talked so Irish, I thought he was Irish. He said, "I have a little school you can teach." I was real glad. There were so many who took "Normal Training" and the state exams, that it was very difficult to get a school to teach.

One day in July mother and I tried to find the school. When we got to this place, which seemed a long ways, there was a man plowing. We asked for directions to the school. I didn't know it was Clarence, my future husband. He told us to keep going, it would be about a mile. When I first saw the school, I felt it was in a beautiful but lonely valley.

When school started I boarded at Dewey Leppert's awhile. Andrew Leppert, Dewey's dad, died before school started. Mother and I went to the funeral, he was buried in the May's Prairie cemetery. I will always remember that a quartet sang, "We'll Never Say Good-bye in Heaven." I felt I couldn't stand it if it were my loved one who had died.

Later that year I came to stay with Clarence and his sister Sadie, who lived next to Dewey. I got sixty-five dollars a month for teaching plus two dollars and fifty cents for starting my own fire. I felt rich when I got my first check.

The school was down the creek a mile from Clarence's home. I was eighteen. I had twelve pupils and a dog, who waited patiently every day until school was out. Attendance was very poor.

The road past the school was very little traveled. If the pupils saw a team of horses, a buggy, a wagon, or a tractor go by, they would start to scream, get out of their seats and run to the windows. It took them a long time to calm down. I don't know if they were afraid of being kidnapped, but the girl who taught the year before I did was also scared when a car or tractor went by.

When it rained I walked with the children who lived across the creek to the place where they had to cross to be sure there wasn't a flood and that they got across all right. I let school out early when it rained. Three of the families lived across the creek. They couldn't come to school if there was a flood. One of the fathers cut a tree and it was laid across the creek, but sometimes it was covered with water. At one time the flood covered the valley between the hills, and the school building was completely surrounded by water.

At noon and recess we had a lot of fun, sometimes playing baseball. Sometimes we used a butterfly net and caught suckers and fried them on an open fire and added them to our lunch.

During the school year I had a box social, and the women and girls brought pretty decorated boxes filled with goodies, and the men bought them. The usual price was two dollars, unless a boyfriend had others raising his bid on his girlfriend's box and he would pay as much as eight dollars for it. The school children gave a short program at the social and the

18

young folks of the neighborhood put on a play. The total amount made was about thirty-two dollars. I bought a little Victrola with part of the money we made from the box social, and a little kerosene burning stove to heat soup at noon.

There was wood for me to burn in the good old pot belly stove, and a sturdy axe for me to chop kindling to get a fire started. Almost every Monday, things were a bit unsettled in the school room, cigarette stubs on the desks and mud on the floor, where hunters had had a little party. The porch door didn't have a key and was never locked. One morning I was sort of dreaming and not wondering if hunters had had a party. I opened the porch door, and my seventeen-year-old pupil, Elizabeth Sullivan, grabbed me and screamed as loud as she could. It is a wonder I didn't have a heart attack.

There were many birds. We had a book that had pictures and literature about the different birds. They became our friends. As I walked to school in the mornings, a chickadee flew from one fence post to the other, waiting for crumbs from my sandwich.

The county superintendent was W. L. Peck, who was superintendent for many years. He said, "Don't let me visit your school and find you aren't playing with the children."

Our teacher meetings were in the courthouse, which is now a museum. At one meeting the superintendent was talking about health, good food, and exercising. He showed us how much muscle he had in his arms and pointed to me to feel his big muscles. It was very embarrassing.

The next year I taught in Franklin township, eight miles from Waukon, but I managed to get home weekends no matter how far I had to walk or how stormy it was. One weekend the snow was so deep that when my folks met me with a team of horses and sled, I fell into the sled, I was so exhausted.

Courtship

For much of the time at Clarence's, I didn't think he liked me, but one night I was on my knees petting their Airedale dog, and looked up at him. His eyes were full of love.

After the little school in French Creek township was out for the year, I went home to help my parents for the summer. In the fall I taught in a school in Franklin township. Clarence would come to see me as often as he could, but a farmer's life is a busy life.

Sometimes on Sunday nights, I wouldn't know if he could come or not. I would sit upstairs and look out the window. I would be so glad when I would see a car coming down the road.

If he came Sunday afternoon, we would sometimes drive to a neighboring town. There is always something beautiful to see. We would often just sit and talk to Mother and Dad and my sisters and whoever was visiting for the day.

Getting Married

Things were a lot different when Clarence and I were married June 12, 1929. Young couples weren't married in a church then. We were married in my parents home, who lived south of Waukon. We were married under an arch of fresh roses that my aunt Lizzie Beall lovingly created. My sister Esther was bridesmaid and Odean Sandry was best man. Reverend Ruben Elliker was the pastor, and Mrs. Elliker played the wedding march. Mother had a big angel food cake baked and a delicious meal prepared.

Clarence asked me where I would like to go on a wedding trip. I said to Pike's Peak, Colorado. It was a busy time to go on a trip as it was haying time. Ferd Buege and Otto Schburt worked at it while we were gone. We went on a bus to the top of Pike's Peak. It was so cold we had to keep passing our hands over our eyelids to keep them from freezing shut. Along the way up there were lakes and beautiful evergreens, on the top it was all ice.

We continued our driving, but I couldn't stand the high altitude and had a hemorrhage from my nose. The blood spattered the windshield. I went into a filling station restroom with my nose bleeding a lot, until I knew he wanted to close. We stopped at a farm home, where the man brought out of pail of ice water and with a dipper kept pouring the water over the length of my left arm, and it stopped the bleeding. I felt very weak.

Although there were some hard things as I grew up, there were many good things. I was glad to have six sisters and parents that loved me. And Clarence. The Lord was merciful to me.

Chickens

During 1929, the year we were married, and for a couple of years afterwards, we raised chickens by setting hens. Setting hens are hens that don't lay eggs any more. They just want to set. We moved these hens out of the chicken house into a different building. We would give them thirteen or fifteen fertile eggs. Sometimes they would set, sometimes they wouldn't. If the eggs were kept warm it would be twenty-one days before the chicks would peep out of the shells. We put each hen in a little house or box on the lawn, and would board it up at first so the little chicks could get out but not the mother hen.

Later we bought a brooder house and stove, but it still wasn't easy to raise chickens. When they were about six weeks old they would pick each other to death. We would have to catch them and dab pine tar on them.

Blocks of Ice

In the 1930s we kept our food cold with ice. The ice box was behind the door in the east wall of the kitchen. Clarence cut ice out of a pond, usually someone was with him. The blocks of ice were stored in sawdust in the ice house.

A block of ice was placed in the left corner of the ice box. It dripped down into a pan underneath. A block lasted more than a day, depending on the temperature.

We made lots and lots of homemade ice cream. We had it for every special occasion and, it seemed, every Fourth of July. There was always someone willing to turn the freezer and someone to hit the chopped ice down and to add salt. The lucky person got to lick the beater when it was taken out.

We also kept food cold with "the icy ball," which was two large balls connected by a curved rod. Every morning the unit was taken to the basement, where one ball was placed on a flame. A tub of water stood by. I don't remember if the other ball was put in that. The unit was carried to the kitchen where the cold ball was put inside the cabinet. The other ball stayed on the outside. It did a nice job of keeping the food cold, but when we heard there were kerosene burning refrigerators, we bought one.

It was nice and tall. There was a freezing unit in the center with trays of ice cubes. One tray held a double layer of ice cubes in which I made ice cream many, many times. The recipe is at the end of this article. I missed that tray long after we had electricity.

The kerosene burner was in the bottom part of the refrigerator. It didn't seem to use much kerosene. It was still working just fine when we got electricity.

Refrigerator Ice Cream

2 eggs	1 c. rich milk
1 c. cream	1 tsp. vanilla

10 tbsps. white syrup or honey, about 2/3 cup.
Some may want to use sugar.

Beat yolks, add syrup or honey. Beat until light and fluffy. Add cream, milk, and vanilla. Mix well and pour in a tray where the mixture will freeze. When firm, add to the beaten (stiff) whites. Keep on beating as you add the frozen mixture by spoonfuls. Return to the tray and freeze.

Telephones

About 1930 we had a phone on the wall, and a crank to turn when we wanted to call someone. Each of us had a number of rings. There were thirteen families on the line, six of the rings we heard, the other seven we didn't hear. We hoped we wouldn't have a long distance call because it was almost impossible to hear, for all the neighbors were listening in to find out the latest news. The operator was kind and would repeat for us. If there was a fire or something important, she would ring one long ring, then we would listen to find out what happened.

One time Bill Buege was here. It was a cold stormy winter day, but he walked ten miles to Lansing because he was thirsty. I jokingly said, "Let us know if you get there okay." To my surprise late in the afternoon the phone rang and it was our nice operator saying, "Bill Buege is at the office here and wants you to know he got to town all right."

Butchering

We would butcher a beef and two or three pigs at one time, usually someone helped. It was delicious meat all winter, but it meant a lot of work. Each time we butchered I canned about one hundred quarts of beef chunks in quart jars in a hot water bath. That meat had a delicious flavor all its own.

We used the sausage stuffer to make rings of sausage; they were put on a pole and smoked. Some years we would cure beef for dried beef. We cut the pork heads in little pieces for head cheese. We also made liver sausage. The bacon pieces and hams were put in a salt brine.

After the butchering, canning, and sausage making was done, we had the unpleasant job of rendering the lard, stirring and stirring the fat pieces in a big kettle until they were liquid. After we cooked the lard a long time, what were called cracklings would go to the top. They were brown and crisp. Some people ate those crisp cracklings, others made soap out of them.

Quilting

Up until the early Fifties we used to have quilting parties. There were seven in our group. We met in the wintertime when there weren't gardens to take care of. We all brought some food to make it easier for the lady who was having the quilting bee. We went to the quilting bee as early as we could, having our morning work done at home. We got there at different times. We felt we had to have the quilt done in one day. It gets dark early in winter months, and we were usually finished by five o'clock. Mothers with small children weren't asked to come. I suppose it was felt it would be too disturbing.

There are two kinds of quilts, quilted quilts and tied quilts. A quilted quilt was a very rare and precious thing. A quilted quilt is sewed by hand with tiny stitches going through the other side. A tied quilt is tied with yarn, putting the needle through the quilt in spaces and tying two knots. We all worked on the same quilt, although then they were regular bed size, probably seventy-two inches by ninety inches. We didn't have queen size and king size quilts at that time.

We cut designs out of cardboard for the plain fabric, tracing around them lightly with sewing chalk so it would rub off. There are many quilt patterns. Most of them are made of tiny pieces of fabric. We sometimes had embroidered blocks, which didn't have a quilted design on them. The embroidered blocks would be all finished, then probably sewed to a block of fabric the same size, then quilted, making a pretty pattern.

Most of the quilt frames were made by the sewing women's husbands. The quilt frames were made from one-by-fours. We tacked the sides of the quilt to the frames with thumb tacks.

I like the quilts with embroidered blocks, set out with a matching color. I like bright, cheerful colors. Some of the quilt patterns are Star, Tie, Basket, Nine Patch, Double Nine Patch, Wedding Ring, Grandmother's Flower Garden, Trip Around the World, Log Cabin, State.

Meals for Threshers

When the grain was ripe it was put in shocks, most people placing six bundles together and a bundle on top to keep the rain from soaking in. The grain was usually oats, sometimes it was barley, which was scratchy and made us itch. Afterwards, the dry grain was put in the huge threshing machine, which separated the kernels of grain from the straw. We expected sixteen to eighteen men when we threshed, and they worked from sunrise to sunset.

For many years Marie Fritz and I helped each other cooking meals. In the morning we would put a bench outside, and place two wash tubs of water on it, two or three basins, a couple of combs, and a mirror.

Some people gave lunch both forenoon and afternoon, the women taking it to the field. We took lunch only afternoons. We would take sandwiches, cookies or doughnuts, coffee and real homemade lemonade. Two or three days before threshing, we would bake two or three batches of cookies. Threshing day we usually had a big beef roast, mashed potatoes and gravy, two or three vegetables, cheese, and always two kinds of pie.

For supper we usually had meat balls, meat loaf, baloney or wieners, escalloped potatoes or potato salad, vegetables, cake, cookies, and sauce.

One time when Clarence was helping thresh at a neighbor's, they were served delicious clover blossom wine. It tasted like flavored sugar water, but after a little, the table began to go around; pretty soon it was going around so fast, it was hard to catch the food when it went by. After awhile, all was well again.

The next big group of men worked on silo filling, then corn shredding. As it got cold, the men got together again to saw wood. If one neighbor worked for another five days and the other one worked two days, there was never anything said about one owing the other.

Home a Hotel?

Sometimes my home seemed like a hotel.

There were two homeless men who came often and would stay sometimes two or three weeks at a time. They would finally leave to go some other place for a little while but would soon be back again.

We were looking at pictures one night, when one of the men was here. Ruth, our daughter, was a beautiful young girl. We didn't know until a long time later that Myron put one of her pictures in his pocket and told people everywhere he went that she was his girlfriend.

We had a lot of agents who managed to come about noon. Every time I saw one was outside talking to the men, I put another plate on the table. It was easy to have one more, and we always had a nice visit.

One time Andrew Wacker was with us at dinner time; he emptied the horseradish jar. We thought he didn't know what he had, it was like a nice mound of mashed potatoes. He enjoyed it a lot it seemed, until the last mouthful.

The telephone repairmen asked if they could eat here. I would have five or six men three days in succession for the noon meal (for several years). They would pay 75 cents a plate. I saved the money and bought a used piano that I still have. When Clarence brought it from Waukon, the hill was very steep by the May's Prairie Cemetery, and he lost the bench. He realized it had fallen out and stopped for it. When the man carried it in the house, one of them said, "This piano is so heavy, you will find it in the basement one of these days."

Sometimes fishermen would stop in the morning, and ask if they could have a noon meal. They were always nice men, they wanted to pay a dollar each.

One time a bus full of prisoners worked down at the creek making hiding places for the trout. One of two men would stop in every morning for drinking water. They were all nice looking young men and I wondered why they were prisoners at Luster Heights. I felt sorry for them and each day gave them a three pound coffee tin of homemade cookies. Later a neighbor asked, "Did you let them in the house?" I didn't have any fear about it.

A couple of years later a man and a pretty girl came to the house. I recognized him at once as being one of the prisoners. He said, "This is my wife, I want you to meet her. I want you to know we appreciated all those cookies you gave us, and I want my wife to see where we made hiding places for the trout. Your neighbors were so good to us, they always waved when we went by. We worked near Decorah later, and they treated us just like prisoners."

I said, "Won't you tell us your name and where you live? I'd like to hear from you sometimes." He said, "We will stop on our way back from the creek." I said, "I will have lunch ready for you." The lunch waited and waited but they didn't stop.

I don't know how long three ex-soldiers stayed here when they got back from the service, Art Swenson, John Fritz and Ronnie Haas. They needed good meals, and to think of other things than war.

I had young folks stopping in for meals a lot when my sons, Howard and Bob, were teenagers. One day it was supper time and three or four extra lads came to eat. One of them said, "I caught a turtle down at the creek, you can fix it for supper." I said, "I don't know how to cook a turtle." He said, "I'll tell you." I ate a little bit, just so I could say I'd eaten turtle.

If we weren't gone, we almost always had a group of people for Sunday dinner.

A German came to the neighborhood, we felt he had escaped prison. He was almost always angry. He would be here a month or more at a time, cutting wood. After he got up in the morning he would walk around the house five or six times screaming. I asked him what was the matter; he said in German, "God in Heaven, the devil for us all. I tell the whole world."

When he would be in the woods working, all of the neighbors could hear his sermons. I didn't feel it was safe to have him in the house, but Clarence felt it was all right, and we needed a lot of wood.

Wolves

There were many wolves in the 1930s. We heard them often in the night. Two or three could make so much noise howling, we wouldn't know whether or not it was a pack of wolves.

One day Clarence was plowing with a team of horses. A wolf followed all day about the length of a car behind him. He felt sure there were baby wolves close by, so he and a neighbor looked in the woods as it was getting dark. They found five baby wolves in a hollow tree. I feel sure they were cute, but the wolves were killing baby calves, so they felt forced to kill them. Clarence said the wolf clawed at the tree and howled the whole night.

Our Delco Plant

We had a Delco plant in the 1930s, which used a wind charger or motor to charge the batteries. There was a wire from the charger or motor to the batteries. The motor had to run when

I used the Maytag wash machine or when I ironed. I had big washes and in those days we did a lot of ironing too. I was always glad to finish so the motor could be shut off. I didn't like the noise, it made me nervous.

Every time we had company, Howard and Bob, our sons, would climb almost to the top of the wind charger. It would sway back and forth. They weren't scared but their mother was. I would say to the company, "Don't look at them and maybe they will come down."

There were twenty-two batteries on shelves in the basement. Our electrician, Max Daniels, came often to check on them and he enjoyed having supper with us. He never married. He liked to hold Ruth, who was small, and would talk and talk to her.

One evening he was checking the batteries. As I was getting supper, I heard a terrible bang. I wondered if our electrician was dead or alive. I opened the basement door just in time to hear a blast of swear words, so I knew he was alive. I don't know what he had done to blow things up but his hands were burned. He rubbed black grease on them. It must have helped because he stayed to eat supper with us.

Hair

Hair styles used to be quite different. For a quick curl we had curling irons that heated in a kerosene lamp. The curling iron was something like a scissors. We grabbed our hair and rolled it after the curling iron was warm, not hot. If we went to a beauty shop we could get a marcel, which was the name of a hair style. The instrument that made it was also called a marcel and was something like a double curling iron.

We also had curved combs. If we fastened them just right in our hair, we would have some waves. We got one of our hair styles by teasing our hair at the ears, until we had a nice round bunch. They were called "cootie garages."

When we first had permanents, the curlers were plugged into a big wheel that hung from the ceiling. The operator had to be careful not to turn the electricity too high. I was told there was a good beauty shop in Decorah, so I went there for a permanent. The girl had the curlers too hot and burned the back of my head. It hurt for weeks, but I was too timid to report it to the shop owner. A lady in Lansing had her head burned by a permanent, all of her hair fell out and not any of it grew back.

Doctors and Nurses

Doctors and nurses didn't have it easy in the 1930s and later. For years Dr. Frederickson and Dr. Thornton were in Lansing. Both of them made many, many house calls both day and night. If one of their patients was seriously sick, they would sit by their bedside all night long. Of all the many times we saw them, neither was ever cross.

When we went to see Dr. Thornton, Mrs. Thornton always came to the waiting room and said, "You can see Dr. Thornton pretty soon." She always had great big bedroom slippers on. Sometimes she would call him about some difficulty, and you had to wait until he came back.

She tried to protect him from being too busy and would sometimes take the receiver off the hook. When we would tell her we tried to call for several hours, she would say, "Oh! I am sorry the grandchildren were here and took the receiver off the hook."

When someone was sick or a new baby was expected, you could have a nurse in your home for a reasonable price. We had a nurse in our home when Roger and Bob were born. We had such a lovely nurse when Roger was born.

Bob was born with baby jaundice, and had a lot of phlegm in his throat. The nurse stood by his crib for hours, watching so he wouldn't choke. She fixed my toast for breakfast before she went to bed at night so she wouldn't have to get up early. I was thankful I didn't break my teeth on the hard toast.

Clarence and I Loved Horses

Clarence loved his big faithful draft horses. We always had six. Every morning before they were hitched up to go to work, they were tenderly brushed and curried, and again at the end of the day when they were through working. Sometimes one of the horses wouldn't like the hired man and would kick him, and Clarence would have to harness it.

One summer we needed another horse so Clarence bought one. She would be in the field working and would suddenly lay down. Clarence would think she was sick and take her harness off, and she would jump up as well as could be, and try to run off. Clarence and the boys, Howard and Bob, didn't like a tricky horse and she was soon sold.

The men were very careful to rest the horses during the hot days. We never lost a horse in the heat. They weren't given water when they were real hot.

There was a lot of sleeping sickness in the horses one summer. Our big, good, faithful Bob got it. The vet, Dr. Saewert helped fix a frame, holding him high up off his feet. He stayed in the frame about a month. The men tenderly kept ice packs on his head to help the fever. He got pretty good again, but had to think a little when given orders to go or stop. Dr. Saewert was a caring vet. The vet before that would say, "I think it needs some whiskey." Then he would say, "I have to see if it is all right," and drink too much of it.

Clarence shipped cattle to Chicago many times, and would go along on the train to see that they were fed properly and given water. One time while he was in Chicago a beautiful American saddle horse was brought from a southern state. Clarence felt she would be a good horse for the boys. A man who had just brought turkeys to Chicago brought Blondie here in his pickup. She was a wild, spirited horse. Clarence felt that if I rode her all winter she would be tame for the boys in the spring. We didn't know then that a spirited horse shouldn't be ridden in winter weather. I had done a lot of riding before I was married, but I was scared of her. Each time before I rode her, I sat in a chair and said the 121st Psalm. Someone would hold her so I could get in the saddle. We only had a poor, small saddle then, an army saddle. One day as I rode past John Weber's farm (next to ours), they started up a tractor to grind feed. Away went Blondie. There was so much snow the ditch was filled with it. She jumped into the ditch and fell. I was thrown quite a ways ahead of her. I ran back and caught her bridle before she could run away. John held her so I could get in the saddle again. I felt pretty sore and stiff for several days. I didn't want the boys to be afraid of her and know that I had been thrown, so I tried to walk nice and straight. She made such a fuss that I didn't try to make her go past Webers again. We would go down to the creek.

We raised two colts, Blondie II and Beauty sired by Alden Larson's stallion that was beautiful, also wild and spirited. Ruth, my daughter, and I rode them on trail rides, but Clarence always worried there wouldn't be a good loading place and they would have a leg broken. We were charter members of the Saddle Club, and I still go to their suppers sometimes.

Clarence and I went to many horse shows and liked the ones at the Waterloo Dairy Congress. We liked the horse shows at West Salem, Wisconsin, too, but we didn't enjoy them so much when walking through the stables. We saw horses that didn't win a prize being punished.

Both Blondie and Beauty were beautiful American saddle horses, but Clarence felt Beauty was special and should be gaited and trained to be a show horse. She was in a training place near Waterloo for two summers. We went to see her one day unexpectedly, and one of the men hired to help take care of the horses was whipping her. We felt awful. Clarence told the manager he would come the next day with the truck to get her. When they got there the next day, they couldn't find something they needed to load her. She knew the truck and jumped in while they were hunting.

We sold Blondie I to Vince Strub. He had a hard time with her, she didn't want him to saddle her. He felt she was the fastest horse he had ever seen. They timed her with a car. She could run thirty-five or forty miles an hour. He said, "I won't believe it that Clara Leppert rode her," but I did.

Ruth and I rode Blondie and Beauty in parades sometimes. They were well matched. Clarence was so proud of them, but they were so scared of all of the noise. They were like unbroken colts every spring. We worried to watch Howard try to tame them. He had a bad back and sometimes they tried to throw him. Clarence and the boys felt they should be sold before someone was hurt. We sold them to friends, Nick and Margurite DeLair of Jamestown, North Dakota. They paid seventy-five dollars each, which was too cheap, but horses weren't selling high then. They kept them a long time and raised several colts. Ruth and I cried as Clarence left with them in the truck.

We Walked in a Circle

The Walsh's were neighbors who lived south of us. About two weeks after World War II started, their daughter Dorothy's husband was killed in action.

Ruth and I were going to walk there to try and express our sympathy to the family. We thought we wouldn't get lost if we followed a fence, but soon there was a huge ditch we had to walk around. If we could have walked straight, it probably would have been a mile, but we had to go around too many ditches.

After some time we saw a house. It was hard to believe it was Orness's house. We had walked a circle in tall weeds. We were full of burrs and tired. We thought we would visit Rose awhile. She said, "Here is a pan, you can pick those burrs off." By the time we had the pan almost full of burrs it was time to go home.

We sent a sympathy card and letter to Walsh's instead of trying to walk there again.

The Methodist Church on the Hill

The little Methodist church on the hill in Lansing township was incorporated in 1858. Clarence's father, Phillip Leppert, was one of the pioneers who helped hew out the stone for the church.

The church was in good shape until about the late Thirties. Andrew Hirth paid the money for a new roof. At times there were services. Sometimes an evangelist would come and there would be a series of meetings at night. Clarence and I went to one of the meetings. The evangelist was walking up to the church as we were. He said, "Tonight my sermon will be on the devil's stick." We didn't know what that was but found out it was the cigar.

The women of the area would meet with the people of the Evangelical Church in Lansing and hold Ladies Aid meetings in our home. The lunch was more like a supper. We often made homemade ice cream. We paid ten cents a month dues.

I think Reverend Prust was the pastor. He called at the homes asking for a little money toward his salary. Some gave him money, others gave him meat, chickens, or eggs. Some gave him oats for his horse. The parsonage was west of the church.

The last time I was in the little Methodist church was probably in 1939. My daughter Ruth was a baby. It was Sophia Frahm's funeral, the church was full. Someone held Ruth while I climbed the ladder to the tiny balcony. The doves flew back and forth cooing, while the minister spoke. Sophia had loved flowers and birds. The doves were trying to say they loved her.

We marvel that the steeple still stays on the church. It is tilted on the southeast corner. Carol Dee said the Lord is holding it up.

Chivari

A long time ago when a couple was married the neighbors would get together and chivari them. We would pound on circle saws, dish pans, and whatever else would make a big racket.

The couple would finally come out of the house and invite us in for a party or give us money to have a party later.

Sometimes the new bride wasn't in favor of the noise and wouldn't come out of the house, and the bridegroom would invite the visitors in for whatever was convenient for lunch, and the men would enjoy themselves.

When Booty Hirth and Abbie Pfiffner were married, we again went with equipment to make noise. We were sorry to learn later that fifty chickens, about six weeks old, crowded in a corner and smothered to death. They couldn't stand the noise. The smiling, happy couple came outside to greet us, and to give our leader some money for a party to be held later.

One time we chivaried a couple in Lansing. It may have been against the city ordinance, but the new couple was a jolly pair, who didn't let the racket last long by coming outside with a gift of money. The Lansing officers were kind and didn't say anything. It was the last chivari party, I was told.

Thanksgiving Days

We had many good Thanksgiving days of which we think often. One time the weather changed our big plans. I had a huge turkey and invited all of my relatives in and near Waukon to come. It wasn't going to be potluck, I was going to prepare all of the food.

I prepared all the food that I could on Wednesday. It rained that night and froze. When we got up Thursday morning, everything was all ice. As we expected, I had to phone that it was too dangerous to try to come. My first thought was, What would I do with all of the food? No one would want to drive very far on the treacherous roads. I wondered if Earl Gruber and his family had plans. They lived two farms down the road. I talked to Clarence, and we invited them to come for dinner. They drove to our place safely. We were glad to have some one share our food, but there was a lot left for other days.

One Thanksgiving we took care of two turkeys, one was for the Saddle Club. We were charter members. For the first time Clarence said it was better to stick their necks instead of cutting off their heads. He tied them to the clothesline that went across the basement. After they were dead, we picked them. The wing feathers were very difficult to pull so we each took a pliers to pull them out. We were finally finished, and let the first turkey down and laid it on the table. When Clarence took the second turkey down, away ran the naked bird, jumping and flying over everything in the basement, with both of us after it. We would almost catch it, but it would fly again. It took us quite a while to catch it. Clarence never suggested sticking a turkey again.

Hunting Coon Was Fun

Men still go hunting coon, and maybe women too, but I don't think they have as much fun as Clarence did. As he worked during the day, he thought how much fun it would be to get a coon that night. Howard or Bob, or both, or a neighbor, would go with him. They usually had a lunch, which was a sandwich or oyster stew before they left, and they dressed up warm.

We never had a real hunting dog, but our plain mutt dogs were good hunters. Sometimes a big forty pound coon wouldn't die right away as expected after being shot, and would drop out of the tree, very angry, to fight with the poor dog.

One night they saw a dog, and when they got closer, found it was guarding its master's jacket. We never knew how long the hunter had left his dog, waiting for him to return. Another night a friendly black dog followed Bob and Howard home. We couldn't find out who its owner was, and felt he was going to stay with us, but one day he disappeared. We felt his owner saw him as he drove by, and put him in his car.

I was always glad when I knew the coon hunters were home. They would drink hot milk or coffee and have toast with butter and jam. It helped warm them up, but I don't think it did much for their cold feet. They didn't care that they didn't have much sleep, they had had a good time.

One lovely, sunny day there was a knock at the door. It was Rose Orness, a neighbor, who had walked here. She said, "I have a coon in salt water, we are having it for supper tonight, come and eat with us." We had never had coon, but we were willing to try it. We were surprised that it was good. She showed the recipe to us. It was long. She said she had to put all of those ingredients in the dressing to make it taste good.

We had a friend who had a pet coon for a long time, it was beautiful. Every time we saw Merrill, the coon was with him. He rode in the front seat of the car like a dog. Merrill never married, so the coon was good company for him. It had its chair at the table every time he ate his meals. One evening Merrill was very tired from working hard all day, and went to the chicken house to feed his precious chickens before dark. He felt, "I can't cry, I'm a grown man," as he looked in horror at twelve dead chickens on the floor and a naughty coon in the corner. That was the end of the coon he had had a long time and had learned to love.

Ole and Rose Were Good Neighbors

Rose Rothermel was married to Jack May. They had one child, Harold. Jack died suddenly. Harold loved working in the woods, and Rose felt she needed help on the farm.

When Dewey Leppert's father went to North Dakota to look after the land he had there, Rose told him that if he met a nice man there, to bring him along home with him. He brought Ole Orness, who was a good and honest person. He was born in Norway and spoke often of his life there, before he came to America. He worked as a hired man at first, but gradually they began to love each other and were married.

One of the first things Ole wanted were pure bred Ayrshire cattle like they had in Norway. He gave each cow and calf a name. I often took pictures of them for him. Ole loved animals. He had a tiny spotted terrier that he patiently taught many tricks. I thought the cutest was when she stood on her hind legs, put her front paws on a chair, and bowed her head to pray. Ole would look at her with loving eyes, he was so proud of her.

Rose was a good cook. She said many times, "Butter makes good things better." Her specialty was sponge cake, which she made often. Her homemade bread was delicious. When she finally had an electric stove, she would fix one egg at a time in a huge frying pan, no matter how many eggs she fixed, so grease wouldn't spatter on her precious stove. She was a careful housekeeper, too. If you had a little mud on your shoes, you left them on the porch until you went home.

She had a squeaky violin. Sometimes when we went there evenings, she would play polkas and waltzes. Ole was so proud of her. As Rose grew older, she felt she was allergic to the lilacs around their home, so Ole had to dig them out. I missed them, it seemed their place looked bare.

Harold, her son, died suddenly, doing the work he loved, cutting trees. I don't think he knew it, but it was found that his heart was on his right side. His wife also died and Ole and Rose lovingly took his four children, Louise, Betty, Adeline, and Carl, into their home. They went to school near French Creek. Carl is married and lives in Waukon. I don't know where the girls are now. Adeline was a tiny baby when born, weighing less that four pounds and fit nicely in a shoe box.

Rose went to town many times with a team of horses and wagon or sled to get feed ground. She always came home about nine o'clock P.M.. At that time we had to go almost two miles for our mail. She would stop at the first neighbor's with their mail, and they would call the next neighbor saying, "Go up to the road, Rose is coming with the mail." I have a shelf unit in my kitchen porch yet. One shelf was for Dewey and Florence Leppert's mail, the other shelf for Ole and Rose's mail.

When Dewey Leppert felt he needed a new car, he bought a very nice one. Once when the road had snow drifts, he left it in Ole's yard and walked home from there. Ole kept his precious sheep in the yard at night, so stray dogs wouldn't attack and kill them. In a few days the wind went down, the snow plow cleared the road and Dewey went to get his nice new car. He was shocked and a little angry to see both doors on one side crushed in. The sheep buck had gone to see what that new thing in the yard was. He saw his reflection in it and thought he had a rival, so he bunted the doors in with his tough head.

One morning I thought I heard a funny noise. I looked out of the east window to see Ole's car in the ditch. He was on his way to a soil conservation meeting. He helped measure land without pay, and urged his neighbors to do contour and strip farming. He must have forgotten for a second that he was driving a car as he leaned out of the window to blow out his nose. Willard Leppert was with him. Willard's window was open, and they were in a bed of elderberries, and Willard's face was splashed with elderberry juice. Willard said afterward that Ole thought it was blood. He looked so worried and asked Willard, "Willard are you hurt?"

Ole and Rose tried to economize, and didn't have a phone. Ole came here many, many times to have me make phone calls for him, as he didn't hear well. One morning he came, looking very sad. He said, "Will you please call the filling station in Lansing and tell them to call the man who picks up dead animals to come for my sheep." I don't know who answered, but he thought I said, "Tell the man Ole Orness is dead." A couple days later Ole went to the grocery store to buy his groceries. It was filled with people doing their shopping. They all looked at Ole like they had seen a ghost. Before Ole could ask why they were staring at him a lady said, "We thought you were dead." Mr. and Mrs. Pat Welch were good friends of Ole, so that day they went to Lansing for Ole's wake. Mr. Saam had a little room off his furniture store where he placed the casket. As the Welches were getting out of their car, someone said, "Hello." They turned to see Ole walking by. They almost fell over in shock.

Ole was going with others to another soil conservation meeting. The car was in the yard, so he hurriedly kissed Rose and went to the waiting car. He was seated but said to the driver, "Please wait a minute." He went to the house and kissed Rose again. When they were near Luana, the car went down a terrible, steep embankment. Ole didn't realize he was hurt badly and helped lift Mr. Marti's body into an ambulance. Ole was in a hospital a long time with a broken pelvis bone. When Rose was told Ole had been in a car accident, she said, "I'm not shocked, he never kissed me twice before when he left on a trip."

In Ole's later years, he developed bladder and prostate trouble and had to have surgery. He didn't have any health insurance. The doctor asked him if there was someone who could take care of him. He said, "Rose isn't well enough, but maybe Clara Leppert would take care of me." I had never thought of being a nurse for a neighbor. The doctor gave me lots of instructions and instead of being in the hospital for a week, he was in our home a week. He was always a good neighbor, I was glad to do what I could for him. As Rose grew older, she tired easily, and asked me if I would wash her four blue dresses that were all alike. I had long instructions on how to wash them by hand and iron them. Our valley seemed warm and sheltered with Ole and Rose living here.

One morning when Howard and Bob went to check on Ole and Rose, Ole was in the house slumped in a chair with a lot of pain. He had fallen on the ice on the porch and had a broken hip. They had an old school bell that they rang when they needed help, but the wind wasn't right for us to hear it this time. After Ole came back from the hospital in Iowa City, he was taken to the home of Chet Barr, Sr., where Mrs. Barr gave him loving care. I took dinner to Rose, giving her enough food for her supper too, but she became too weak to stay alone and both she and Ole were taken to a nursing home in Cresco. We were awfully sorry that they were taken so far away.

Ole's birthday was in March, so Clarence and I took a decorated cake to him. We looked out of the window, and there was a real snow storm. Ole said he would like for us to stay longer, but he was worried about us driving home in the storm. He was always thinking of others. He told us that with the small amount of money he was given every month, he had bought a stone at the Lansing cemetery for Rose and him. Rose didn't live long. Ole lived about four years after Rose died. After he was in Cresco awhile, he was taken to West Union, where it was so far away it was difficult to see him. Clarence and I were probably about the only ones who did go.

Dixie Was a Good, Faithful Dog

Our daughter, Ruth, married Andy Beyer. We kept their little dog, Ginger, for four years while they were in Beirut, Lebanon. Andy is an engineer. When they came home to Houston, Texas, and took Ginger, Clarence felt very lonely and I felt we should get another dog.

I was on my way to Lansing one day when I heard an ad on the car radio: "Spitz dogs free." A couple of days later I drove south of Waukon to see the puppies. Only one puppy was left, she was white, tan and brown. She was nursing her mother, a pure bred white Spitz. The father was a terrier. I felt she was cute. Five inches of Dixie's tail were white.

I asked Irene what I should pay her. She said, "I don't want you to pay anything, please take me out for coffee some time." She didn't drive. It was in the fall, I was busy freezing the food from the garden. I felt so busy I sent her a check instead of taking her out for coffee. She and her son were killed in a car accident a couple of years ago. It is my regret that I didn't forget about being so busy, and did not give her a nice afternoon out to lunch.

I don't remember Dixie playing with dog toys like most puppies. When I let her outside in the morning she would hunt mice and sometimes not come back for an hour. She sat on Clarence's lap most of the time for two years, and he would talk soothingly to her. After Clarence had a stroke, it seemed she was too heavy, and he didn't want to hold her anymore. She would lay behind him as he sat in his favorite chair, and growl when anyone came near him. At night she would sleep at the foot of his bed. He developed pneumonia, and we took him to the Lutheran hospital in La Crosse. Dixie missed him so much she chewed his bedroom slippers to tiny bits before he came back.

We took care of Clarence for three years, as he continued to have strokes. We had a hospital bed so he would be comfortable at night. Howard and Bob were wonderful, lovingly getting him out of bed mornings and wheeling him to the chair he loved, in the wheel chair. Ruth did all the things she could the times she came to visit. Barbara, Bob's wife, and Della, Howard's wife, were also dear, helping in many ways which I will always remember. The grandchildren also helped lovingly.

Dixie would always watch every night as Howard and Bob put Clarence to bed. She didn't want anyone to touch his blankets. They couldn't resist teasing her sometimes, and she would growl at them.

Dixie seemed to realize when we took Clarence to the hospital for the last time. Lesa, Josey, and Audrey, Bob's daughters, tried to hold her but she pushed the screen door open and followed us to Howard and Della's, where their dogs chased her back home. She was a lonely dog for a long time. She slept on a big rug in my bedroom and became my watch dog. If any one came in the house at night, she stood at the top of the stairs alerting me that someone had come.

One evening an insurance agent came at 9:30 P.M.. I told him I didn't like agents to come in the late evening. She didn't like him and stood by me growling at him. When he finally left, I tried to keep her in the porch, but she pushed the screen door open and chased him all the way to his car. He was very angry and growled at me to call my dog back.

She continued to be my watch dog until she couldn't hear well anymore. I will always think of Dixie as a wonderful little dog, there will never be another dog like her. She was seventeen or eighteen years old when she died.

Closing Thoughts

This is the closing of my book. I had never thought I would be writing stories for a book. I want to thank Robert Wolf for his kindness and patience as he watched for my mistakes. I hope I haven't hurt anyone in any way, but as you read of the "simple times" of the past, may there be some small thing that will help you in some way. All of us have had some hard things in life, but we try to think of all of the joy we have had.

I thank the Lord for my loving family, Bob and Barbara, Ruth and Andy and Della, my ten grandchildren and their husbands and wives, and my ten little great-grandchildren, and all of my dear relatives and friends.

May the Lord give all of you many "special" blessings and to all who read this book.

Thank you. With love, Clara.

Part II:

BEFORE DIESEL

The stories in this section first appeared in *Voices from the Land* and *More Voices from the Land.*

RICHARD SANDRY

Richard and Dorothy Sandry arrived at the workshop several months after it opened, recruited by Greg Welsh. Richard's facility impressed everyone, but Dorothy informed us that years ago he had written love poetry for her. That first evening he wrote a piece on threshing, then disappeared for the winter. Then, sometime in the spring, Richard unexpectedly arrived at my home, bringing this piece.

Memories

It stands alone now and largely unnoticed by the numbers of people who pass by it every day of their busy lives. Like a giant old oak tree that is removed from the scene, it would not really be missed, unless for some reason, one day, the building would be gone. Officially it was known as Lansing No. 3, but to most it was known as the Churchtown School.

Its life has been stripped from its interior: the students' desks, the teacher's desk, the recitation bench, and all the material that set it aside as a place of learning for those first wonderful eight years of elementary education. Its bell having rung to call the children to its doors for the last time some thirty-five years ago, its only purpose now is to serve as a monument of brick and mortar to by-gone days. Days of a slower pace of life, when terms like 'substance abuse,' 'AIDS,' 'government programs,' 'government deficits,' 'welfare programs,' and 'abortion' had not yet come into being.

Built in 1875 on the highest spot in the nearby area, it commands a panoramic view of the hills and valleys dotted by farms and homes. Some of the farms are now empty and their buildings mostly abandoned because, due to the government's cheap food policy, their owners could not make enough money to support their families and had to move on. These same farms in earlier times were prospering and sending sometimes six or seven children to school, all at the same time.

Due to the lack of records we have to use our imagination and fantasize that maybe the builders of the school somehow stored away a spirit in her. Maybe in the belfry or perhaps behind her two large blackboards. What stories she could tell of nature's elements beating against her walls like so many armies trying to knock down the walls of a fortress. For nearly one hundred and seventeen years she has won every battle, and stands as sound as the day of her completion.

She would remember her first teacher telling the students about then-President Ulysses Grant and of the Civil War and President Lincoln's assassination just ten years before.

She also heard firsthand of current events like the Spanish-American War, the sinking of the Titanic, the first automobile, the first airplane, World War I, the great depression, World War II, and the Korean War. The time span of fifteen presidents from Grant to Eisenhower.

I wonder if she would remember that first day of school in the late summer of 1941 when a shy, black-haired boy entered her door for the first time to begin his eight years of education. He soon learned the advantage of being the first one to school on those opening days in succeeding years, not because he was so anxious to begin the year, but because that usually gave him the pick of his desk for the year. The best one being the one by the window, where if the teacher didn't notice, he could look out of the window to see which neighbor was passing by with their team of horses or which one was going by with their new Farmall H or M or John Deere A or B tractor.

The old building would surely remember the students preparing for the Christmas programs for weeks before the big evening arrived. That evening all the parents and many others of the community would come to see the program of "pieces" and plays. The final instruction being to speak loud and clear so the people in back could hear. This was all followed by a gift-exchange and a two-week vacation.

She would remember the row of bicycles parked by her wall in the spring and fall and the coaster sleds in the winter time. Also the row of dinner buckets ranked in the hall waiting to be opened at noon and sometimes their contents traded or bartered for something in someone else's bucket. Also the large water cooler, which was filled every morning by two of the older boys going to the creamery with a can and bringing back the day's supply of drinking water. This was an enjoyable twenty-minute trip.

When nature called, the procedure was to raise one's hand and ask, "Teacher, may I leave the room?" Permission granted meant a trip of about forty yards to the outdoor toilet. Funny, but nature always seemed to call more often in the nice days of the spring and fall than it did when it was thirty below zero in the winter time.

Heat was furnished by the one large register in the middle of the floor, which also necessitated an outside trip to the side door to stoke the old furnace with coal. The last day of school in the spring was also a big occasion, as that day all of the mothers would pack the picnic basket with goodies and the fathers would stop their work long enough to come to school so everyone could enjoy the picnic dinner. After a few games were played, the parents would take the children home with them to begin the summer vacation. That day brought talk (with mixed emotions) of whether there would be a new teacher for next year.

Now back to reality. Fifty years have passed since that day in forty-one. The boy has grown to be a man, the black hair has mostly turned grey, and as he drives past the old school he looks into that same window, smiles, and says to himself, "Old school, thanks for the memories."

Black and White

by Richard Sandry

What is the earliest recollection in your life? The one that really stands out in my mind happened in the summer of 1939. I had just turned four years old. I remember my dad had been painting some of the outbuildings on our farm when he had time, in between all of the necessary things that had to be done on the farm. How nice they looked when he was through painting them. They shined a bright red and the corner boards and all of the trim boards and window frames were painted white.

Our car was a 1929 Model A Ford. Originally it was black, as were about ninety percent of the cars in those days. The rest were a drab, blackish green. From setting outside, the paint on ours was very faded, and a lot of rust was showing. Dad had said many times that when he finished painting the buildings he was going to paint the old Ford. I could just picture how nice the old car was going to look when Dad finally got around to painting it.

I remember this particular day. The sun was shining brightly, and it was beautiful. The old car was parked in the yard, and my dad was busy in the hayfield. Now, of course, I was too small to be helping him then, but as a four year old I really wasn't too busy. At least I didn't have anything planned that couldn't wait for another day. That was when I got this terrific idea. Why not help Dad by starting to paint the car? I really don't remember why I chose the white paint over the red, maybe it was just more accessible. I had just finished the left rear fender and was standing, admiring how nice it looked now, a shining white instead of that dull, old black, when Dad came home from the field for dinner. He didn't see me or my painting until he walked around the car on his way to the house. I don't remember the look on his face, but I wish I could. All I remember was him calling to my mother in the house, "Come quick and bring some rags."

I stood behind my mother while he soaked the rags in gasoline and washed the still wet, white paint off. Dad was a very mild-tempered man, so to my benefit I was not punished. It wasn't too long after that that he finally got around to getting the car painted a shiny black. Now, I wonder if the Detroit engineers had seen my work if history might have been changed. Maybe they would have turned out black cars with white fenders or white ones with black fenders.

Threshing

by Richard Sandry

When you are ten years old and can be along with the men on the threshing crew, it can make you feel pretty grown up. The threshing ring then consisted of about twelve neighboring farmers.

Sometime in July when the oats fields were all a golden yellow, it was time to cut and shock the grain. The grain binder was brought out from its year of rest in the machine shed and was pulled by five strong horses, or in later years by a tractor. The fields then turned from yellow to a shade of green as the oats were cut, tied in small bundles, and deposited in rows on the ground by the binder. Usually this was done on some of the hottest days of the summer.

The oats bundles then had to be picked up by hand and shocked. A shock was usually six bundles set on the ground with one bundle laying horizontally on top, called the cap. Many farmers liked to do the shocking in the cool of the evenings, sometimes keeping on until midnight. For the next two weeks, the shocks went through a sweat, or drying time.

It was then time to begin threshing. Each farmer would bring his team of horses and his "basket rack," which was a large wagon box to hold the bundles. Some had tractors hitched to the wagons. It was necessary to move along the rows of shocks to load the wagon. This is where I came in as a tractor driver. This was a big help to the man who was loading the wagon, as he did not have to crawl continually on and off the tractor. To be able to drive those early tractors was quite a thrill for a young boy.

The bundle wagons were then brought, one on each side of the threshing machine, and the bundles pitched into the machine, one bundle at a time. The machine separated the oats from the straw, the oats coming out of a spout and put into sacks. The sacks of grain were then hauled to the granary where they were emptied. The straw was blown onto a pile which was called the straw stack.

Dinner was always something to look forward to. Three or four of the farm wives would go together and cook the noon meal. It was served family style with all of the men sitting around the table. When the men were eating, there was plenty of kidding and telling of tall tales, which really held my attention. I'm sure my dad did not share my enthusiasm for the threshing, as for him it meant a lot of hard and sweaty work, but for a ten-year-old boy it was the big event of the summer.

CLARA LEPPERT

I repeat this piece from Simple Times *because it complements Richard Sandry's piece with the woman's point of view.*

Meals for Threshers

When the grain was ripe it was put in shocks, most people placing six bundles together and a bundle on top to keep the rain from soaking in. The grain was usually oats, sometimes it was barley, which was scratchy and made us itch. Afterwards, the dry grain was put in the huge threshing machine, which separated the kernels of grain from the straw. We expected sixteen to eighteen men when we threshed, and they worked from sunrise to sunset.

For many years Marie Fritz and I helped each other cooking meals. In the morning we would put a bench outside, and place two wash tubs of water on it, two or three basins, a couple of combs, and a mirror.

Some people gave lunch both forenoon and afternoon, the women taking it to the field. We took lunch only afternoons. We would take sandwiches, cookies or doughnuts, coffee and real homemade lemonade. Two or three days before threshing, we would bake two or three batches of cookies. Threshing day we usually had a big beef roast, mashed potatoes and gravy, two or three vegetables, cheese, and always two kinds of pie.

For supper we usually had meat balls, meat loaf, baloney or wieners, escalloped potatoes or potato salad, vegetables, cake, cookies, and sauce. One time when Clarence was helping thresh at a neighbor's, they were served delicious clover blossom wine. It tasted like flavored sugar water, but after a little, the table began to go around; pretty soon it was going around so fast, it was hard to catch the food when it went by. After awhile, all was well again.

The next big group of men worked on silo filling, then corn shredding. As it got cold, the men got together again to saw wood. If one neighbor worked for another five days and the other one worked two days, there was never anything said about one owing the other.

BARB LEPPERT

Barb is well respected in the community as a fourth-grade teacher. She works on the family farm as well, helping her son, Andy, with morning and evening milking. Like the others in the group, she has great resources. Her sketches help give readers an idea on the nature of daily farm life.

Horses vs. Tractors

The horses were already gone when I came to live on the farm, so I don't have any firsthand knowledge, but I have heard a lot of stories from my husband and his parents.

The horses were worked pretty hard for an hour or so, and then they had to be rested. The woman of the house, knowing this, could plan for the noon meal to be done to coincide with one of these rest periods. The horses were brought in and watered and fed, and only then would the men come in for their meal. They would sit down to chicken, mashed potatoes and gravy, corn on the cob, coleslaw, fresh baked bread (that you could smell all the way out to the field), and a big slab of juicy apple pie. After devouring this meal they would go outside under the big shade tree in the backyard, sit down in the lush green grass and tell stories or jokes until the horses were sufficiently rested.

In contrast, today, when I have dinner prepared and ready at noon, it might be 1:00 P.M. or later before Bob comes in, because he wanted to get that field finished or get all the hay raked so he could bale it later in the afternoon.

He hurriedly eats his dinner with one ear glued to the radio to get the latest weather forecast. No one dares to talk while he listens. If there is any rain in the area he jumps up, heads for the door, and gets back on the tractor that didn't need to be rested or fed anything but gasoline!

FRANCES COLE

Frances Cole contributed to Voices from the Land *under her earlier name, Frances Geinzer. She is a hearty woman, who with her husband, Danny Cole, raises sheep and cattle.*

R.E.C. for the Country

It was a wonderful thing when rural electrification was put in for farmers and ranchers. We got our electricity in 1945. First we got the buildings all wired, then, gradually, got appliances to do the work easier. Of course lights came first, doing away with kerosene lamps and lanterns. One of our first installments was a milking machine, doing away with milk stools and pail. Then to go along with it was a milk cooler and an electric separator, as then we sold cream. Times were not too good in the forties, and you just bought electric items as you could afford them. My uncle in Chicago got mother her first refrigerator, doing away with the ice box, where a large chunk of ice was set in every day. That kept everything cold until it melted.

Sometimes I wonder how we could ever go back doing things without R.E.C. All water was pumped with the windmill, and sometimes when the wind didn't blow water got low. I remember a few times we put a gasoline engine on the well and pumped water that way. Then again, in the years before R.E.C., hardly anyone would have been able to pay the monthly light bill. I know in winter when days are short, with the electric tank heater going and the tractors plugged in so they will start, bills get really high. But as long as we can afford it, we wouldn't be without it.

The Tornado

by Frances Cole

May 22, 1962 is one of the days in my life I will never forget. It started like any other day with our morning chores. It was corn planting time, and my husband went to plant early that morning on one of our far back farms about two miles from home. Around noon the weather became very hazy and sultry and very still. We all kept working at our daily chores, but my mother said, "Start your chores and milking early, something bad is coming out of this weather." She was always afraid of us being in the barn when it was storming.

Well I, my aunt, and the man who was working for us got done and were out of the barn by 6:30 P.M. The sky was threatening and so dark and hazy. We all went to the house for supper. My husband was home from corn planting by then.

Well, after supper we done up the dishes and about 9:00 P.M. everybody was heading for bed but me. I had a bowl of gold fish and started cleaning them. I went outside to throw out the bowl of water and rain drops like spoonfuls and very hot were coming down, and it was so dark you could not see the hand before your face. I hurried inside, and just as I came through the door a gust of wind blew dirt right behind me. I rushed to the stairs and called to the folks to run for the cellar, something was going to happen. Well, we did. I was the last one down the stairs and could see through a window. Everything got real bright and it sounded like a freight train was going through the yard. Well, that is when it struck, then all got deathly quiet.

We finally went upstairs and rain was coming down the back stairway, a window was blew out and we got a big piece of cardboard to nail over it. Well, then mother looked out of her bedroom window, and that is when the nightmare began. Everything looked bare outside. We could see lights we never could see before.

I and my husband went outside and had to walk through the front yard as all the electric wires lay in the yard. The windmill lay only a foot from hitting the house. Our red barn was flat, tree limbs all over, pigs were squealing and calves were bellowing. The only light we had was in the house, all the others were out. Mother called some of the neighbors and one came over. We worked with the power saw freeing calves and two Angus bulls we had just bought. One had his leg injured and had to be sold, five calves were dead, as well as one sow and many young pigs. A sheep had a foot cut off and some geese were killed.

Well, when daylight came we found we had lost seven buildings. Our sheep shed we never did find. And everything had damage to some extent, except our tool shed and two brood coops full of young chickens. Seems crazy, but by 11:00 P.M. the stars were out. It was a beautiful night.

Next day, lot of folks helped salvage things from the wreckage. Our milk cows got so frightened they took out a section of cowyard fence and we didn't find them until the next day. A system to milk them was set up in the old barn and we struggled with that all summer. By August a new barn was up and slowly we got back to normal, but no one knows what cleaning up after a tornado is like until they go through it. I know I will never forget.Barb Mitchell

BARB MITCHELL

Barb and David Mitchell joined the workshop during its second year, just prior to making their decision to quit farming. Barb has worked at a nursing home for some time, in addition to raising four children, two of whom, Peter and Emily, came to almost all the workshop sessions.

Aprons

I remember when aprons were important to all women. Everyone wore them, including my mother.

A few years ago I went to a birthday party with my sisters, cousins, and aunts. There was a table full of aprons, and we were told to pick one out and wear it. We were to think about it, and at the end of the party tell a story of what kind of an apron it was. It was interesting what came out of it.

Also to help us think we played a game of writing down the uses of an apron. Can you think of any uses for one? My mother answered that question many times over the years, and I had to think.

Mom's apron served many purposes. They kept her dresses clean, covered up missing buttons, or a dirty dress. There was always a clean one handy in case someone drove in the yard. At times she had several on. They brought garden stuff into the house, held eggs gathered from the chicken coop and more.

As little kids we often got an "owie." An owie is when we got a finger or an arm, a toe or a knee hurt somehow. Mom's aprons were always big enough to cover it or wrap it up and hold it closer to her. It always got better. The grandchildren often came to her for something.

There was always a pocket, and in it were many things. A button found laying some place, a hanky for anyone's nose or cut. Often there was something for the grandchildren to reach in and take out. They loved it.

She played peek-a-boo with many babies with her apron.

If it was a bad day she threw it over her face to cry, and no one would know it. It wiped many tears from all of us. Sundays brought out good ones as company often came back then. My aunts would come visit with one on.

Mom had a wringer washer back then. I often watched and later used one myself. The apron strings often got caught in the wringer. Round and round they would go before Mom popped open the wringer to free them.

It was my job to take down the washing from the lines after school. Have you watched the wind blow the apron strings? It was as if they were constantly trying to free themselves or to reach further. Sometimes they were around the clothes line and had to be unwound in order to take them down. Back then they were ironed and folded just right. I'd always run my finger over the string to unwind it again.

There were many different kinds of them—full ones, gathered ones, fancy ones, and more. A long one always came up to the chest with a loop over the head. It was tied at the waist like gathered ones. A gathered one was usually gingham and covered the bottom half of their dresses. Other kinds of aprons were used too. Waitresses at weddings wore fancy ones. Now you see them in restaurants. Cooks wear them, butchers wear them.

Maybe you can think of more uses or kinds of aprons. My girls enjoyed playing house with them. At kindergarten the kids paint with one on. So there are still some uses for aprons today. But with automatic washers and dryers it is easier to take care of them. Can you remember Mom or Grandma with one on?

DOROTHY SANDRY

Although Dorothy only showed up at the workshop once in 1991-92, when she wrote this piece she returned on a frequent basis to the next year's meetings.

Bluebirds

I have always enjoyed watching birds since grade school days when my teacher hung a bird feeder outside the window of our country school.

Some years ago in the spring, my husband came in from the pasture and told me he had seen a big flock of bluebirds. He made two houses and hung them for me. We watched and waited but no bluebirds came. The years went by and every so often I'd read more information on bluebirds.

About six years ago we decided to try again. We made eight new houses and hung them along our country road. I'll never forget one forenoon I heard a bird singing, and I came and looked out the kitchen window, and there sat a bluebird on the framework of my bird feeding station. Most of our houses were occupied by bluebirds that year.

We enjoyed it so much that the following winter we made more houses, so we now have twenty-four, which I check every seven to ten days, and record how many eggs each nest has, how many hatch, and how many fledge. Each fall I report these figures to a volunteer of the Department of Natural Resources. Since the bluebird was on the endangered species list, they keep records from anyone who will report to them.

Since the decline of people using wooden fence posts, the bluebirds lost a lot of their nesting places. They are increasing in numbers now due to people and organizations putting up houses for them.

I really look forward to making the rounds of our bluebird trail. If my husband has time he joins me, for he enjoys it nearly as much as me. One year we recorded a bluebird nest with pictures, beginning with the eggs and ending with the young birds nearly ready to fly. The mother bird was very protective of her eggs, so we also got a picture of her sitting on the nest.

We can often look out onto our lawn and see one bluebird or several at our birdbath or on the lawn looking for insects.

We have learned so much since we put up those first two houses years ago. The biggest problem we had was that something was getting into the nest and pulling it apart, destroying the eggs. Often we'd find adult feathers laying on the ground. For several years we lost a lot of nestings. Finally we figured the culprit was a raccoon. I made a phone call to an Urban Nongame Biologist with the DNR and she sent me information on what to do.

One suggestion was to put several small dowels on the inside front of the house a little way down from the entrance hole. The idea was that the dowels would stop anything from being pulled up toward the hole. That did not work. So next I made a hardware cloth cone measuring three and a half inches wide, five inches tall, that extended six inches out from the box. This was stapled onto the front of the house over the hole. We bent the outer prongs of the hardware cloth out so there was a sharp edge all the way around.

Success at last! Last year we had no more problems with the raccoon. We fledged eighty-six bluebirds and are looking forward to their return this spring.

Part III:

FARMING TODAY

The stories in this section first appeared in *Voices from the Land* and *More Voices from the Land.*

ALICE MCGOVERN

Alice was never a member of the rural writing workshop, but wrote this in another Free River Press writing workshop in Lansing, Iowa, whose purpose was to document life in that town. This selection is from a book an her first experiences in rural Iowa.

The Arrival

As I stepped off the train at 8:00 P.M. in Prairie du Chien, I was shocked by the dimly lighted platform and station. It was drizzling rain, and Larry, my new husband, said, "Wait here with the luggage while I go around the corner to the garage and get the car."

Having always lived in a big city, and now, having traveled from Pittsburgh to Chicago, I had never experienced any place so quiet, small, and dreary. The station master turned out all the lights.

Jacquie, my nine-year-old daughter, and I huddled together, scared of the silence and darkness following the Zephyr's departure. There was a big, old house on the opposite corner from the depot. On the first floor porch a dim sign flashed, saying, "Beer." We could see men near the bar where a big fat woman was serving drinks. There were five men at a table playing cards. A couple of women were watching, and laughing with them.

Larry packed our luggage into the car. I had six bags to be followed by two trunks being shipped. Once in the car we passed through Prairie du Chien's business district. So this was Prairie du Chien, Wisconsin! The French name sounded very exciting and sophisticated. Larry had told us that this was our destination on the train. It wasn't exciting. Not this small place! It was only two blocks long. There was a small bank, a shoe store, and a garage in the first block. The next block had a machine shop, a grocery store, another garage, and a fish market. The store that caught my eye had a sign, "Star Department Store," over a small store front. I couldn't believe it. Macy's and Gimbel's were department stores, not that little old room.

It is about three miles across it." We heard the bridge groan, and the clickety-clank as the car went up on it. It was a very old bridge. It seemed to be complaining about the heaviness of the car as we traveled through the thick foggy mist that hovered over the river. As the car left the bridge I thought, "At last we are in Iowa. I sure don't think much of Wisconsin. I hope Iowa isn't as desolate."

As we traveled the highway with the dark, forbidding Yellow River Forest on one side and the Mississippi River on the other, it started to pour rain. A few miles up into the hills we turned onto a dirt road full of chuck holes and I thought, "How well did I know Larry? This must be a mistake." But then I saw a sign saying "Harper's Ferry."

I thought, "At last, a town. Oh! Yeah! Six lights. Oh, boy! So this is Iowa."

It was so damn dark. Nine miles up the road Larry took a sharp turn down a hill, got out, and opened a crude looking gate.

I thought, "Where's the house? Don't they have lights? Oh, my God, what have I done?"

When Larry got back into the car I said, "Nice place for a murder, no one would ever discover it."

Larry was shocked, but he answered, "It is really a beautiful place in the day time, Alice."

It was one-half mile to the house, and Larry hurried me into the dimly lit kitchen, where his father was washing dishes or maybe the separator pans. Grandpa said, "So here's the cook."

I thought, "Hmmm. That's why he came to Pennsylvania, to find a cook. All those sweet-talking words about how beautiful I was, all those presents and candy just to get a cook. And I fell for him. I'll never forgive him. Never, never, never."

Grandpa was in working man's overalls. I thought, "Daddy never wore such clothes, and look at his mother in those men's pajamas. She has a skin disease. I can't believe this horrible situation — and I'm married."

Grandma (Larry's Mom) said, "There are sheets in the hall closet, and your little girl can sleep on the couch in the living room."

"Oh, no," I said. "No one is leaving Jacquie downstairs alone. We will sleep downstairs, she goes upstairs." I wasn't going to leave her unprotected in this wilderness. No doubt they thought I was crazy.

Larry and I had spent our honeymoon at the Lee Hotel in Washington, D.C., and my aunt Mamie had Jacquie at her home in Petersburg, Virginia. We didn't want Jacquie to be jealous of Larry, so we took her back to the hotel for a couple of days of fun.

Once we got to the farm we bought new beds, and I divided my time between the two of them, sleeping every other night with Jacquie, until at the end of ten days Jacquie told me that her single bed was too small for me too.

Life on the farm was quite dull. Their radio was only turned on when news was on, or if Grandpa wanted to listen to a ball game. There was no TV, which I had had for four years. La Crosse didn't have a TV station yet. The old folks resented my city ways and intrusion into their life. Larry was forty years old, the oldest of their family, and here was this widow and her nine-year-old daughter expecting all his attention.

Grandma used to say quietly, "So-and-so was away in the service, but he came back and married a nice girl from around here." After repeating it over and over, and praising my sister-in-law from Waukon, I finally was fed up with all these little digs, and exploded. "Don't you think I'm a nice girl? Well, let me tell you here and now, I'm twice as nice and ten times more intelligent than most girls around here."

The Coming of Machinery

by Barb Leppert

With the coming of the age of machinery came long hours in the fields and consequently the loss of yet another old and valued tradition...that of visiting neighbors.

When there were only horses to pull the machinery, farmers could only work just so many hours, and then the horses had to be rested. The chores were done at the same time every night, and that left ample time after supper to go visit a close neighbor for the evening to play cards or whatever. It was fun. You never knew when someone would pop in, but it seemed like you always had some fixin's in the refrigerator for lunch.

Now when the field work starts you might see your husband at mealtime, unless he decides to take a sandwich and an apple along to the field with him, in which case you will only see him for five minutes when he comes in, washes up, and falls into bed exhausted. He falls asleep two minutes after his head hits the pillow, so if you have anything you want to talk over with him, you'd better talk fast.

This ritual goes on during the planting, cultivating, and harvesting seasons. Then one day you come home from work and he's sitting on the steps with a big smile on his face and he says, "I'm done with the first crop hay.

58

Let's celebrate and go out to eat. Why don't you call Betty and Curt and Donald and Eleanora and see if they want to go along?"

That's about as close to the old time visits as we get anymore. But that's the price we pay for progress!

DAN BYRNES

Dan Byrnes, who joined the workshop in its second year, farms outside Waukon, Iowa. Dan, who is in his thirties, went to college and later worked in Minneapolis, but returned to his native state to work with his father on the family farm.

The Silo

In the 1920s my grandfather, John Byrnes, built a silo thirty feet tall, fourteen feet in diameter. The construction method was very similar to the method used today: cement staves one foot wide, two feet long, and two inches thick are set side by side in a circle. Metal rods or bands are then wrapped around the outside to support the structure. The inside is covered with plaster to keep the silo airtight. At the bottom of the silo, where there is more pressure from the stored silage, there are more rings. On my grandfather's silo the rings near the bottom were spaced two feet apart, and near the top, three feet.

The silo was located next to the barn. Each year the unit was filled with chopped corn silage. The filling was done by neighborhood crews. Corn plants were cut by hand, loaded on flat wagons, and then fed into a machine at the silo that chopped the plants up and blew them through a pipe. The corn silage was then fed to the cows during the winter. Each day someone would climb up in the silo and use a fork to throw down the needed amount. The silage was carried to the cows with a basket. In the dead of winter the silage would freeze to the sides, so an axe was used to chop it out. The silo worked well for about forty years. As farming changed, the silo became too small.

In 1961 my father and uncle built another silo, located about fifty feet from the old one. In 1971 another silo was built, this time sixteen by sixty. In 1979 a fourth silo went up. Sometime in the seventies they quit filling the small silo. Too much labor for too little capacity. The wooden doors rotted out, and the staves began to crack. Near the top a few staves were ready to fall out. My cattle loaf beside the silo, and in order to prevent an accident we decided to tear it down.

At the Barn Restaurant in Prairie du Chien there is a series of photos of a man knocking out staves with a maul until the silo toppled. Another man from Viroqua, Wisconsin won ten thousand dollars from "America's Funniest Home Videos"—one hit from a maul and his silo came crashing down.

I have absolutely no experience in tearing down a silo, but on Thursday night at 7:00 P.M. we started, my father and I. We decided to knock out a stave on each side, thread a cable through it, and then pull with a tractor. My dad is in his seventies and does not swing a maul much; he does drive a tractor. We went out to the silo with cables, chains, a tractor, and an eight-pound maul. The top staves looked like they could fall at any minute. What would happen if I hit a lower stave? Would the vibration cause an upper stave to fall? My dad said he would watch above, and if he yelled, to get the hell back. I beat a hole in each side, threaded the cable, and hooked up to the skid loader. My dad drove forward, and the tires spun on the cement. Two big black marks were left. We went for another tractor, the sixty-five-horsepower loader tractor. It left bigger marks than the skid loader. The silo did not budge. Next we hooked up the one-hundred-horsepower International tractor. More black marks. My dad backed up and took a run at it. The silo did not budge. Maybe after seventy years here the silo had learned the Byrnes' trait of stubbornness.

Time for a new plan. My idea was to cut one of the metal rings. My dad got the skid loader, loaded the oxyacetylene torch, and parked safely inside the barn next to the silo. I stood next to the silo with the torch. The band exploded with a bang as I completed the cut. Again my dad pulled and again the tractor just spun. We cut another band. This time I was prepared for the band to explode out, and I ran away after the cut was complete. My dad pulled again. This time the staves on the south side started to move. We wanted an even pull so the structure would fall between the fence and the barn, not on them. I took the maul and beat out the staves on the north. The remainder of the staves pulled out easily, but the silo still stood. With a four-foot hole in the side going halfway around, it looked like a monster ready to bite into anything that came near it, or at least smash a skinny farmer who was foolish enough to go near it.

Then my dad thought up a plan: go up and knock out a stave behind the third band up, and then hook up the cable.

Unsafe? Yeah, but most of farming is unsafe. I walked up, took a swing and then ran back, out of the way. Then I hooked up the cable. My dad got in the tractor, I stood way back. The silo came down with a crash. Dust and rocks flew like a bomb had just exploded. In a few minutes the dust settled, and the silo was now just a pile of broken cement and iron. At 8:30 P.M. we quit for the night.

All of the material from the silo will be re-used. The staves will be used as base material under new cement, and the metal bands will be used for concrete reinforcing bars.

The silo project is just one of a long string of facility repairs that we have done since I started to farm in 1987. My dad and I are builders. Many evenings are devoted to fixing facilities. We are proud of the fences we have built, the buildings we have fixed, and the concrete yards we have made. The sense of accomplishment after building something is great, and the facilities make our livestock work easier.

My grandfather would probably not recognize the farm today, but I hope that he would approve of the changes.

Would You Believe It?

by Richard Sandry

Saturday afternoon, and it has been a beautiful day. The sun has shone all day, the humidity is low, and it's the kind of a day when you can look around and enjoy the beauty of all of the surrounding hills.

I am sitting in my combine, really enjoying my job. Everything is running smooth as silk. In about an hour I will be done for the season. I think it would be a good evening to go home, take a shower, and take my wife out for the evening meal. My thoughts are momentarily interrupted by a small squeaking noise. Well, I think, that can't be too serious. But soon I find I was very wrong, as within seconds the small squeak turns into a big squeak, then a loud bang, and right before my eyes the large auger on the header has just twisted into two pieces.

This means hundreds of dollars in repairs again, something we sure didn't need. Instead of that relaxing evening I had planned, we decide to save the money and figure out what to do next. After a night's sleep we decide to try to find someone willing to finish the field and postpone the repairs until next year.

Monday afternoon brings straw baling and again everything is humming along fine. One more load, I tell my son, and we will be done. He takes the previous load to the barn to unload, and I start on the final one. After about ten bales the pickup on the baler stops turning, something has broken inside. I take the baler to the machine shed and tell my son to go get the big baler and finish with that.

He is just about done when I see him stop. Upon inspection we find that a bearing on the big baler has "gone out." So much for that. This leaves a windrow of straw about fifty feet long in the field.

In relating this story to a friend I tell him that we were going to take the pitchfork and pick up the rest of the straw. "I wouldn't do that," he says. "You probably will break the fork handle."

BOB LEPPERT

Bob was one of the first organic farmers in Allamakee County. He is a man who thinks and questions, and is open to experience. Most farmers resisted the invitation to the workshop, Bob found it intriguing. As someone noted about most of the group, they are striving to express ideas, not trying to be literary. Bob's work, like that of the others, is of a piece with the rest of his life.

Farming

The first farming I was able to do when I was growing up was to help take care of the chickens: feed them, get the eggs, and at night make sure they were all in the coop with the screen door closed so foxes couldn't get them. I was too small to harness the horses because the horses were so big. My brother was three years older than I and he could get them on by himself. Everything, the plowing, discing, and planting, was done by horses. We had our W-30 McCormick Deering tractor, but it was only used for providing power to grind feed, thresh grain, and shred corn because we had all horse machinery at that time.

I can remember when planting corn I would help move the planting wire for the planter. It had buttons on it and would be stretched all the way across the field to be planted. The planter had a guide to hold this wire while going across the field, and each one of the buttons would trip the planter to drop the corn in the ground, so that when we cultivated the corn, we could cultivate it the long way and also go across the field to help control the weeds.

Chemical fertilizers, herbicides, and insecticides weren't available yet. About this time, hybrid corn became available and would be standing in the fall when it was time to harvest. This was unreal, because the open pollinated corn seemed always to be laying on the ground. My hands would be so cold when we had to pick the ears out of the snow. I would keep asking if it was time to start chores so I could get to the house and warm up.

About this time we got our first rubber tire tractor, a two-cylinder John Deere B, with a brake for each rear wheel, which was really an improvement to help it turn in loose soil. This tractor would run on power fuel, which was similar to kerosene. The tractor had two fuel tanks, a small one to put gasoline in and a large tank to hold power fuel. When the tractor was cold it had to be started on gasoline and switched to power fuel when it was warmed up. I can remember the fuel man filling our fifty-five gallon tanks in the shed. There were no pumps on the truck and he filled five gallon cans and carried them in and emptied them in the tanks, each time moving a lever with numbers on the rear of the truck to keep track of the total amount of fuel delivered.

As each year went by, Howard and I would pester Dad to cut the horse tongues off the implements so we could use the tractor on them. Also, we kept buying more machinery as it became available after the end of World War II. In 1946 we purchased a new John Deere A tractor with a two-bottom plow and cultivator for $810.00. Then came the fifties and with it, chemical fertilizer, herbicides, and insecticides. I remember the first year we used a herbicide: the instructions were not followed correctly and we had corn that year, no weeds, but it was four years before anything else grew on it. We never did use any pesticides because we only had corn one year in a field, then it would be rotated to oats and then hay for the next two years.

In the fifties we purchased our first diesel powered tractor and a four-row corn planter and cultivator. During this time, the popular statement was, if you are having financial problems, get bigger. My brother and I would buy every calf and pig we could afford and then some. We would rent farmland even if we had to drive five miles to get to it. We worked day and night to get all the work done. We did this all through the fifties and sixties. By the time we got into the seventies we were so big we were having serious problems getting money to keep going. We had passed the limit at our local bank and were getting money through them from two other banks in the cities.

About this time we had grown with our cow-calf operation to two hundred and twenty cows. Then two farms we had been renting were put up to auction and we figured we couldn't afford to purchase them. The next year the State Conservation Commission notified us that it was terminating the leases on the land used to pasture our cattle. We were very disgusted and in the spring of '72 we took a hundred and fifty of the cows to the sale barn. As I look back now, it was the best thing that could have happened to us. The cattle sold good and we were able to lower the amount we had borrowed quite substantially at the bank. This was the first time we were able to pay off rather than borrow. We changed our cattle operation around and sold yearling calves rather than finish them out to fat cattle for slaughter. We found as we got smaller that our profits increased. Better efficiency meant less interest to pay at the bank.

About 1976 I got invited to a dinner meeting put on by the Wonder Life Corporation and got introduced to organic farming. There were a couple of farmers there who had been farming this way for years, but I couldn't believe that this could work, even though I thought it was a good way to farm. So I had to try it. My brother, Howard, was not very interested in the idea, but we decided to try it on fifteen acres.

The Wonder Life Company had a program and recommended that a chisel plow be used instead of a regular moldboard plow and that a soil inoculant be used, which helped get the soil back in condition. The first spring after we had used the soil inoculant we noticed lots of angle worms again. The way we had been farming, using the chemical fertilizers, few could be found, even though we never had used any insecticides.

We kept increasing the number of acres cropped with this new program, even though my brother was not too interested. Our yields were not as big as when we used chemical fertilizers, but our costs were lower. The soil improved in texture, too, and became more like a sponge, taking less power to till. As a result, the farm ponds around the edge of the fields in the pasture started to dry up because the rains would soak in, rather than run off.

One drawback we discovered was when chopping corn in the fall to fill silo, we could only fill the wagons half full because they would sink into the mellow soil and we would be stuck. My son, Andy, was big enough by this time to pull loads to the silo, and when he came home one evening from helping our neighbor fill silo, I asked him if he had problems pulling in the loads of silage. He replied, "Dad, their fields are just like concrete. Never got stuck once." Our neighbors had been using lots of fertilizers, herbicides, and insecticides, and the wagon tires only made prints on the soil.

About this time my brother Howard's two boys were out of high school, and we decided to divide the partnership. When we divided up the farmland, I got one hundred and eighty acres next to the home farm, and got to rent the home farm, which is three hundred and fifty-five acres. The farm is owned by my brother, sister, and me.

For the next six years I didn't use any chemical fertilizer or herbicides, and I had good crops. Once while I was getting the strips evened out to the same number of acres, I did something I was told not to do. I put one strip back to corn for the second year. It was a failure. The corn didn't grow good and the weeds came. I chopped it for silage, but there wasn't a good ear of corn in the field. Since that time, I have used some organic fertilizer, which helps get the corn up and out of the ground sooner so I can cultivate. I do use a small amount of herbicide if we get a rainy spring, and I can't get out to cultivate.

All the new equipment and devices to make work easier on the farm have a price tag attached. As I look to the future with my farming operation, I can see the day when I will have to decide either to borrow huge sums of money to purchase replacements for worn-out equipment, or quit farming altogether. I've been getting along by purchasing used equipment and repairing it, but even this old used equipment is getting scarce and the price is getting higher because of the high cost of new equipment.

My 4020 John Deere that I purchased new in 1964 has ninety-five horse power and cost $4,700. Today a new John Deere tractor with the same horse power costs $42,000. My round hay baler cost $3,100 in 1972; the same baler today has a price tag of $26,000. The field chopper which cost $1,800 new in 1956, costs $26,000 today.

I have been getting along with my old equipment because I have a small farm, and I make most of the parts for this old machinery when it breaks. I have to, because most repair parts are not available any more from the machinery dealer.

If I could only get a fair price for all the food I produce, I could make some machinery purchases which would help the hometown people and would put many people back to work in the factories again.

High Interest Dilemma

by Barb Leppert

The hardest thing for me to understand when we were first married and raising our family was the high interest. Every year when we'd figure taxes, I'd say, "Bob, look how much money we could have in the bank if we didn't have all that interest to pay."

He'd say, "Yes, Barb, but we have to borrow money to pay bills until we sell the cattle. We can't just let those people we owe wait for their money."

We were not into dairy then. We had a big check once a year when we sold cattle, but by the time we paid off the bank loan and the interest, we were right back where we started. In a few weeks, Bob would come in and say, "Well, we need this or that and we don't have the money in the farm account to pay for it."

I'd think, "Here we go again. Just once I wish we could be out of debt."

It wasn't until thirty years later that I finally realized that dream. Our kids were grown up and gone from home by that time, but they were as happy as we were when we paid off the bank.

Bob's brother, Howard, and he were in partnership with their dad so everything was on thirds. Because our cash on hand was so minimal, we lived on a third of the egg check, which varied from $5 to $25 a week. From that money we bought things that we couldn't raise ourselves. We had our own meat, eggs, milk, and canned or frozen vegetables. Believe it or not, I was even able to save a few dollars out of our third each week until we had enough to go out for a special treat with our four children.

Life might have gone on this way for years, but my teaching certificate had to be renewed by the next year, because I had graduated in 1955 and mine was a ten-year certificate. I had to get six hours of credit in my chosen field. I went to summer school with a group of teachers from the local school system. Toward the end of the summer, they mentioned how much good substitute teachers were needed. They encouraged me to apply. I talked it over with Bob and my mother-in-law, who lived across the road from us. She and my sister, who lived in Lansing, would babysit our children. The substitute pay was $15 a day. I gave the babysitter $3 of that.

The next year a fourth-grade position opened up. The salary was $4,500 a year. To us that sounded like a fortune. Our oldest child was in the first grade and our youngest was just two years old when I started back teaching. The thing I liked most about this profession was that I was home at the same time as the kids. We had the same vacations and everything. Bob always said the money I made teaching helped keep our heads above water.

We have had to borrow money from time to time since, but it doesn't seem to be as threatening to me now. I am still teaching, and Bob gets half of the milk check every two weeks, so we can pretty much stay on top of things.

ESTHER WELSH

After helping with farm work and raising eight children, Esther entered college, earned her L.P.N. degree, and now works part-time in a nursing home. Like many others in the workshop, she surprised herself and pleased the rest of us with what she wrote.

Getting Started

As our farming career was about to begin, I saw that our major assets were our hopes, our dreams, our faith in God, a lot of ambition, and family support. Bill's only possession was a 1953 Chevy, and I had nothing but a small savings account. I was working in the office of a local factory, and Bill was working in a gas station just to get by until we could start farming.

Bill used his free time to go to farm sales, hoping to find the bargains and buy some of the essential farm equipment we would need. Then moving day came. Our household furnishings consisted of wedding gifts, family extras, and a new refrigerator—one with a foot pedal to open the door. Our local implement-appliance dealer said it hadn't been a big seller, so we got a bargain. A big, rusty, round oak stove, standing near the back entrance was to provide our heat. As the March winds blew through the house and water began to freeze in the kitchen sink, we came to realize that we needed another source of heat. We merely mentioned to my dad that our water pipes had frozen and that we even had ice in the dish pan. Soon we had an oil burner that they weren't using. Oh, how nice it was to be warm again!

For early spring field work we borrowed a tractor, a plow, a disc, and a planter, either from Bill's family or mine. We planted a garden, but I know we harvested more out of our parents' gardens than we did our own, and much of it came in jars.

Money was always in short supply and the cupboards were often pretty bare. Oatmeal was our staple. We didn't have a lot, but we didn't have much debt, either. When our first load of pigs was ready for market, we planned our first celebration. We invited Bill's brother, Dan, and his wife, Sarah, to have supper with us. All four of us squeezed into the cab of the pickup and took the pigs to market, then went to buy groceries for our celebration. We bought a chicken, potatoes for french fries, and bakery bread. We all worked together to cook supper. It was a fabulous meal. I can taste it yet.

In time, the rented farm where we began our career was sold, so we moved to the farm where we live today. This farm was owned by my uncle, Bill, and he had been renting the farm because of failing health. Now that we had more land, we bought more cows, and more feed. A brand new John Deere 60 tractor was delivered, which cost us $2,215.00. To us that was a lot of money at that time, a major debt, but this past year a major tractor repair cost over $5,000. By the time we bought the cattle, the feed, and the tractor, we were well indoctrinated into the process and need to borrow money. When I would get nervous and wonder how we were ever going to pay that money back, Bill would re-assure me by saying, "You can't start farming without borrowing money." Oh, how true that was and still is!

Our record keeping was simple those first years. Unlike my uncle, who kept his receipts in a shoe box and recorded checks and deposits on a long stick and merely got another when the first one got filled, we tried to keep a record of all farming and household income and expenses. We find those records interesting yet today. For example, in 1955 we paid $193.80 for a new foot pedal refrigerator, $25.80 for a used wringer washing machine, and $9.15 for a pair of bib overalls for Bill—the same brand that cost $21 to $23 today. That same year, market pigs brought $15 per hundred weight; today we are getting $40 to $43 per hundred weight. Prices have increased, but so have costs, so it seems we merely handle more money.

As time goes by, our hopes and dreams may change a bit, our ambition may fade, but we continue to see God in the things we do and in the people we meet, and we know that we all need one another.

Choices

by Esther Welsh

My husband, Bill, and I have shared over thirty years of farming experiences. During each of those years our plans and ideas have changed frequently. We dreamed of the good life, we planned, we studied, and we worked. We looked to our elected officials, to the universities, and to the Extension Service for information and advice and sometimes were misled.

We consulted nutritionists and feed dealers to help us develop rations for our livestock to get the best rate of gain. We depended on seed dealers and fertilizer salesmen to recommend products and amounts that would produce the best quality and highest yields. There were so many things to consider. Then we had to weigh the information and make the best choice possible and yes, we made some mistakes. Mistakes that often became more obvious and more serious over time.

Our farming operation grew bigger and bigger. We rented more land. We tried new products as they were introduced. With more land and more work, it was essential that we find ways to cut corners. There was no time to cultivate the corn three times. There was no time to study the needs of the land or the livestock. There was no time for family fun.

And then came the eighties. For many farm families and small businesses those years will be remembered as truly hard times. The value of our land, our equipment, and farm production slid to a devastating low, while farming input costs increased and interest rates climbed to a high of twenty-two percent. Those same capital investments that we had planned for, and that appeared sound to us only months before, had now become unmanageable debt.

Financial difficulties and forced decisions are painful. Feelings of defeat, depression, and desperation cast a cover of gloom over farm families and farming communities. At the time, we were raising beef cattle and pigs and sliding backward financially at an accelerating speed. When the cattle and pigs went to market, they were scarcely bringing enough to cover our cost of production. There was no profit, yet there were bills to be paid.

There was work to be done but there was little enthusiasm. Our minds were struggling with choices; our hearts were aching over forced decisions. Everyone in the family was feeling the tension. We were all willing to work hard and long. We were even willing to do without, to ask for less, but who in their right mind wanted to work ten to eighteen hours a day and still fall short on payday? We needed to find alternatives. We had to make changes. If we thought that things were bad we were soon to realize that it was only going to get worse.

We were completing some definite plans to cut back on land, inventory, and work load. At the same time we were making giant strides toward changing our farming operation from conventional to chemical free. We had a confirmed order for twenty-five hundred chickens if we could raise them without using antibiotics and without hormones to hasten their growth. We had always raised chickens for our own use, but this was a sizeable difference. We were confident that we could do it. We were excited about the opportunity. Finally our plans were coming together.

Then one day early in March, my husband, Bill, suddenly began to complain of a tight feeling in his chest and of shortness of breath. He was anxious and restless. He was rushed to the hospital where he was to remain for three days. After extensive testing, he was told that he could go home and do what he felt like doing, that he was as healthy as a twenty-nine year old.

Three days went by, and all was well. Our niece and nephew had come to spend a few days. Our daughter, Jeanne, a nursing student, was home from college, so we invited friends to come for supper. I was just putting the finishing touches on our meal when again Bill began to complain of tightness in his chest and shortness of breath. He said, "Just get me some oxygen, and I'll feel better." Our son Gary had the car running, and we convinced Bill that there was no time to waste. We went back to the hospital.

This time the diagnosis was heart attack, and was followed by three weeks of hospitalization and more tests. Finally on April 3, his birthday, Bill was released from the hospital with orders to *rest*, not to lift over five pounds, and to eliminate stress.

That was sound advice to insure recovery, yet it seemed like unrealistic advice for a farmer in the spring of the year, but again there were no choices.

Our son Gary managed to seed the oats, and planted the corn that spring too. Under different circumstances he might not have been allowed such an important responsibility. This was Gary's big chance to prove himself capable. There were many offers of help and support, a real benefit of living and working in a small community.

Not all the decisions we made throughout the years were well planned. Some were made in an instant, but at the time we felt we were making the best choice possible. Our farm and farming is important to us and to our family. We consider it a privilege to produce food, a basic need for all mankind. We are proud and excited to tell the world that we can and are producing crops and livestock without using synthetic chemicals and antibiotics. We are confident that the choices we have made so far will help to preserve and protect our land, our water, and our environment for our own use and for generations to come.

GREG WELSH

Greg is an all-rounder who can run a food co-op, as well as farm machinery. He also writes impressively. A man of ideas and energy, he is the one Iowa state extension agent advocating organic farming.

Forced Auctions

They gathered at the auction, harmless buzzards, strangers, neighbors, friends, relatives, patiently waiting, watching as the farmer's lifelong collection is sold.

"All right boys, what do ya want to give for it boys?" the auctioneer spouted, as the disc, plow, wagons, and tools sold to the highest bidders. Children wandered about, oblivious to the liquidation of their future.

Forced auctions, like an Irish wake, finality on the one hand, a neighborly respect to those passing on the other. No one asks why. It hurts too much. No one denies, it wouldn't be right.

Farm Crisis

by Greg Welsh

Through the eighties, each day the evening news reported a crisis still lived. A farm crisis, a human crisis, soundbites of emotional turmoil, forced auctions, and white crosses. A time of desperation, marked by suicides and fear, unnoticed by most.

The daily newspaper reported farm suicides and rural stress like that day's fatal car wreck, corporate buy-out, or weather.

What happened to agrarian wisdom? There's an auction, and another, and another. One more farmer sells, then another, and another. Then what? Then what?

Storm Clouds

Two years after writing this piece, Richard quit farming.

by Richard Sandry

It is a nice warm June afternoon. The sky is a robin's egg blue with the white cumulus clouds lazily drifting on their way to their rendezvous with the horizon. A gentle breeze ripples my short-sleeved shirt as I gaze out over the cornfield. Knee-high already and the deepest dark green you can imagine. I think about all of the money we borrowed and all of the planning and time it took to get that crop to where it is now.

My son comes to my side. Now my mind drifts back to when I was his age and I stood beside my father looking at the results of his toil those years before. Then I think, is this the end of the line? I think of how farming has changed over my lifetime, of how we have progressed to where profits are practically nonexistent. What has he to look forward to should he wish to farm? I am filled with a deep sadness and fear for his future, as I have seen an interest in raising livestock and working with the soil being nurtured in him, maybe even bred right into him. "Let's go to lunch, Dad," he says.

This brings me back to reality, and for the moment I forget the future and the past. I look to the west and see the dark ominous storm clouds rapidly moving upon us. "We had better hurry," I tell him, "or we are going to get wet." In the back of my mind I remember something being said on the radio this morning about storms coming this way.

We finally get home and just as we come into the house, the rain begins to fall. Shortly the full fury of the storm is upon us. As I watch, looking out through the window, I think of how the days of my life go. How the clouds on the horizon of my sunrises sometimes, later in the day, turn into the black clouds of fear, of despair, of anger, of uncertainty, and of depression.

As suddenly as it began the storm ends. The corn is bent but not broken. Soon the sun will come out and the corn will straighten and begin to grow again. I think how a turnaround in the farm economy would revive the farmers, make them refreshed with that spirit and vigor that has always been a farmer's attribute.

Tonight I will thank the Lord for seeing me through today and ask for guidance for tomorrow. With spirits bent but not broken.

The Day of Reckoning

by Dorothy Sandry

My husband and I are at the sale barn. We have brought in our fat cattle to sell, our main income for the year. We have a farm payment to make, a note due at the bank, and other payments depending on the sale of these cattle.

We sit on the bleachers that surround the sale ring on three sides. The sawdust covered ring waits for the first animal to be brought in. The buyers are sitting together in one group. I'd seen them together before the sale in the sale barn cafeteria having coffee together. They had probably already discussed with each other how many head each one needed, so they wouldn't need to bid against each other too much. Scattered here and there among the crowd of around seventy-five people, I see other cattle producers. It is evident from the caps advertising seed corn, fertilizer, and feed that most of the crowd are farmers. I also see retired farmers who came just to pass the time. The air is becoming thick with smoke and, as they start bringing in the livestock, dust mingles with smoke.

The gate opens, and first they bring in small calves that are one week to a month old, one at a time. As each one is sold, another gate opens, and the ring man chases the calf out and bangs the gate shut. Next, they bring in the cows, with or without their calves at their sides. Then they start to bring in the fat cattle, in groups of one to around twenty, depending on how many that individual farmer had brought in. The fat cattle are separated by their size, and heifers are separated from steers. There is a scale in the sale ring, and they are sold by their weight.

Our nerves are on edge as we wait for ours to be brought in. Finally, the first group comes in. The ringman moves them around in the ring. The auctioneer starts them with a bid and gets no response. He lowers the bid, and finally the bidding starts. But wait! He said, "Sold," and that isn't enough! Three more groups come in, and the same thing. They're sold, but it isn't enough to pay all those bills already due, and those coming up in the future. We knew the price was down, it had been for three months. But the cost of the feed we bought to feed them was up. The cost of hamburger in the grocery store wasn't down. The fuel for the tractor that put in the crop of corn and made the hay for them had gone to near record highs. Why must we always take what they want to give us for what we have to sell? No other business can run that way. If we could figure our costs and labor on top of the value of the cattle we had sold, we and all the area farmers would be able to help keep the local businesses going. Now, as it is, we get by with as little as we can, and rural towns are dying.

DAVID MITCHELL

Unlike many farmers, David Mitchell is willing to express his thoughts and feelings about the stress of farming.

Diary

Monday, February 15, 1993

Not much time left before the sale. Damn phone, I feel like taking it off the hook. Every time I sit down, it rings. See, it's ringing again. This time it's our daughter, Donna, from Ames. She's excited about having a teaching interview in Farnam, Nebraska. She wants me to look it up in the encyclopedia to locate the town.

After looking at the road atlas, and not finding it, I tell her that I will look it up in the encyclopedia like she asked me to, and call her back. Explaining the location, and encouraging her to go, I tell her I wish the farm sale was over so I could drive her there. We talk some more about the distance and whether Mom will be able to rearrange her work schedule and drive to Ames and take her over. I say, "I'll check and have her call tomorrow."

As we say our good-byes my mind goes back to the farm and the sale, especially the accomplishments and failures of the last twenty-seven years that we farmed. Sure glad I have the record books for all twenty-seven years.

I spend the rest of the evening adding some of the totals. I want to know how many pigs we had finished for market in those twenty-seven years, so I go through each account book, one for each year, '66 through '92, and add the totals. Approximately twenty-two thousand. I feel proud of myself for that.

Now for the bad part, the interest paid. One hundred eighty-one thousand dollars for twenty-seven years. Then I break it down to the eighteen years that my brother Jerry and I were in partnership together, and the last nine, when I farmed alone. Thirty thousand dollars for the eighteen years in partnership, one hundred fifty-one thousand dollars for the nine years alone.

Tuesday, February 16, 1993

Our daughter, Lisa, came over from Viroqua today to help us get things ready for the sale. Her daughter, Kelly, was with her. She sure is growing fast.

I got Lisa busy with cleaning the small addition we call the mud room. We plan to use it for the checking of the sale.

When Lisa was done with the mud room, I asked her to clean the combine windows and the inside of the cab; there's plenty of dirt and dust in it. It hadn't been cleaned since before we combined the oats in July. There is oats chives still on the floor. She done a wonderful job with both tasks.

A lot of people were still calling to ask about this or that piece of machinery, so I did a lot of running back and forth to get my jobs accomplished for the day.

I had no idea that there would be that many people calling, if any, to ask about the machinery or the cattle. I had never done it myself when I went to other farm sales to buy some item we needed.

We were learning many new things about a farm sale, by our firsthand experience. I knew there was a lot of work to prepare for it, but the task seemed to get bigger, and it seemed I wasn't gaining much ground.

Wednesday, February 17, 1993

More phone calls asking about the machinery. Sure am glad there are a lot of people interested.

Dan Cole came over today to help get machinery out and lined up. I took the tractor and blade and bladed the snow off the field below the buildings, the only somewhat level area on the farm. Hard to blade the snow into windrows, because of the volume of snow we have. That reminds me, they are talking about more snow for the weekend. Dan and I started putting the pieces of machinery in two rows in the field. I really enjoyed working with Dan. A lot of machinery was frozen to the ground. I was afraid we might break something getting it loose.

Barb called us in for dinner. More phone calls. I took it off the hook for awhile so I could finish my dinner.

I know that I made some wrong moves, buying some of the machinery too soon or not figuring what it would cost to own it per acre of use. I guess my desire to own things or the greed got carried away somewhat.

The pain to own these things or the extra work to service the debt was getting too much. I see now that the writing workshop was the power or the people I needed to help to come to grips with my situation.

Thursday, February 18, 1993

Dan came again today to help. James Moore and John Gibbs, two other neighbors, came too. My brother Billy came out from town.

There was some repair work I needed to get done on the corn planter. It took a lot of our time. Jim made a trip to Eitzen for parts. It was a busy day getting more equipment to the field, even with all the help. But it keeps my mind from all the worry. Thank you, God, for neighbors.

Friday, February 19, 1993

I went to Eitzen after chores, for oil filters for the 8010 and stopped at the vet's office to check on test results for the cows. I was kind of worried. Three of the cattle did not test clean the first time, so the vet retested them about a week ago. Thank God they tested clean.

After supper I spent some time answering the telephone again. A man from Wisconsin called about one of the D17 tractors. As we talked I sensed he needed someone to talk to him, so I did. There sure are a lot of stressed farmers. Lord, what do we do to help?

Saturday, February 20, 1993

More people came throughout the day to look at the machinery. It really kept me busy with taking time to talk with them and getting the work done. Jeff Sweeney came later in the afternoon and helped a little. He also helped write up a contract for renting the pasture.

Sunday, February 21, 1993

We went to church and to breakfast this morning. Laid all the things that were bothering me before the Lord. It's great to know him and have a place to go when things get too much for us.

Lots of new snow today. The weather man says it's going to keep coming. I'll spend most of the day pushing it around and grading it off our driveway, which is one-half mile long. These next two days are going to go fast with the extra work that the snow makes.

More people came and called again today. I'm starting to feel I'll be glad when it's over. I think I'm starting to burn out again.

Monday, February 22, 1993

Lots of new snow. There must be at least fourteen inches. Dan and Billy came out to help again today.

The county sent a man with a maintainer to widen the snow on the driveway and plow snow off the field north of where the machinery is lined up. The windrows of snow are six feet high in some places. It was quite a job even for the maintainer.

I really worried about Dennis Weymiller's sale that was scheduled for today. Lord, sometimes the crosses are more than we can bear. My nerves are beginning to bother me, and I'm getting grumpy.

Barb went to the bank for us today to get the titles for a couple of the vehicles we're selling.

Tuesday, February 23, 1993 *Sale Day*

I'm up early for once, for one of the biggest days of our lives. It seems there is a week's work left to do before the sale.

Really glad it's going to be over soon. Most of the days I felt I was running around like a zombie, rushing and stopping to greet someone, now and then.

It looks like it's going to be a great sale. Lots and lots of people, hope there's going to be enough parking for them.

Doug, Eddie, and their hired man, Paul, came. The swatter wouldn't start. Paul got it running just before the sale started. It's damn cold. We got the last of the tractors and self-propelled equipment started so it would be warmed up for the sale.

It was good to see a lot of people out from town too.

I was really glad when it was over. Some things could of brought more, and others brought more than I expected.

Sunday, January 2, 1994

Wow! Almost a year has gone by since the sale. Not all sunshine, but some roses—you know they have thorns.

Some of our farmer friends are calling me lucky for not being in farming during the '93 planting, growing, and harvest seasons. I keep telling them someone had to pay the rent.

We didn't sell the farm, we rented it out. The land that we didn't rent out to the taxpayers through the CRP program we rented out to neighbors.

We still have our income tax to pay for '93. Hopefully we can refinance the farm to pay that.

It's like they say, the longer I've been away from full-time farming the less I want to go back to it and be a slave to machinery and other things. I've tried sales and learned a lot about it. I will probably do some of it in the future. I presently deliver bulk propane.

Part IV:

STEWARDSHIP

The stories in this section first appeared in *Voices from the Land* and *More Voices from the Land.*

BRUCE CARLSON

Bruce is a dentist who works conscientiously on local community projects. In his free time, depending on the season, he gardens, bikes, skates, or skis. He also practices zazen, or Zen meditation.

Soil

I was not raised on a farm, but farming and the soil have been a part of my life. Living on the world's largest fertile plain has had an impact on me. The texture and feel of soil in my hands has been a powerful connection to the environment for me since I was a boy working in my parents' garden.

I was raised in Ames, Iowa, home of Iowa State University, one of the original land grant colleges. These institutions have shaped farming practices for over a hundred years. In the late sixties and early seventies, when our society was in turmoil, the government and these agricultural institutions felt the need to expand U.S. agricultural exports to feed the world and bolster our economy. Farming techniques that had been evolving for centuries were put aside and the genetic engineering of seeds and the heavy use of chemicals became the way.

Looking back, if we would have developed sustainable agricultural technologies for export, the world's food supply would be light years ahead of where it is today.

To save and build the soils we have left, is what organic farming is about. There were a few farmers who followed their instincts and never left crop rotations, wind breaks, and the many practices that farming fence-to-fence with lots of chemicals and big equipment seemed to make passé. It must be hard to be a sustainable farmer and see the majority of your colleagues throwing chemicals everywhere and reaping short-term profits from exploiting the land.

The turmoil between generations that the sixties produced was very evident in organic farming. It seemed that organic farmers were hippies with long, dirty hair living in a commune. This image was promoted to the point where it would have been un-American to see any value in anything these people believed in.

If the universities had promoted the values of the Aldo Leopold Center for Sustainable Agriculture, instead of following the advice of pro-chemical lobbyists, like the former Secretary of Agriculture Earl Butz, the hippies would have only been on the fringe for their lifestyles, not their farming practices.

To see the corruption and greed of corporate America creep into our soils has been hard for me. When I watch soil run thick as chocolate down an erosion rill, I am sickened. Taking for granted and abusing this precious ingredient to life is a sin. I find it hard to believe that even a hundred years ago, when soils were so thick it seemed they could not be depleted, that a farmer would not have been saddened to see the destruction of his fields from the power of one rain storm.

We speak of tolerable soil loss. Why do we farm on a limited and depletable medium and speak of its demise as tolerable? Why do we tolerate non-sustainable agriculture?

I have lived on the banks of the Mississippi River for fourteen years. The power that a river is, the energy in moving water, may be why I love this ecosystem so much. The soils from the hills that surround this mother of all rivers have literally been choking the life out of the water.

The realization that farming practices are the reason for the river's demise has been hard for me. I've always felt the Corps of Engineers was the dirty culprit by diverting as much water as possible away from the backwaters into the main channel. To see chemically laden silt choking these backwaters is wrong, yet we have done almost nothing to stop the practice of tolerable soil loss that has led to the depletion of life within this river's ecosystem.

I feel the way we treat our soil is so indicative of how we feel about our planet and the ecosystem we live in. Could it be that if we changed our thinking about soil loss not being tolerable, air and water pollution not being tolerable, human suffering and corporate greed not being tolerable, that all life on earth would be sustainable?

Image of Farmers

by Esther Welsh

My mental picture of a farmer is a man dressed in bib overalls or blue jeans, a chambray or flannel shirt, sturdy high top shoes and a hat that advertises for the local machine or seed dealer. He carries a pencil and a small notebook in his pocket to help him remember appointments, record the number of pigs per litter, the date a new calf was born, or the variety of seed he planted on the west side of the road and in the terraced piece.

Today we commonly see pictures of farmers wearing one-piece coveralls, plastic gloves, plastic boots, and plastic eye protection. That is what he needs to wear to reduce his exposure to chemicals— those same chemicals that we apply to the land which directly produces the food we eat or produces the feed for our animals, which will eventually provide the food we eat.

Is this a sign of advanced technology in the clothing industry? Is this advancement in agriculture, or suicide for healthy family life?

What about that farmer in his overalls and chambray shirt who for years applied those same chemicals to his land without the protection of the spacesuit-type wardrobe; who ate his lunch in the fields with the same unprotected hands that had handled the chemicals as they were being mixed and applied to the land?

What about the nine-year-old boy who spent five days of his summer vacation in the hospital, desperately sick with high fever, swelling and extensive rash that was diagnosed as an acute inflammatory disease (Erythema Multiforme), cause unknown?

What about the farmer whose hands and arms swell every spring while he is applying chemicals?

What about the farmer who grows his crops without using synthetic chemicals, yet watches the chemical drift travel through the air as his neighbor's corn field is being sprayed with a herbicide by a hired commercial sprayer because he doesn't have time or doesn't want to cultivate?

What about the cost to that farmer who pays for commercial spray application but loses valuable product to the atmosphere as the country breezes carry it through the air?

Yes, we farm men and women are always looking for new technology to save time and make farm work easier, but how much are we willing to

84

pay? How much are we willing to sacrifice? How long are we going to ignore the research that assures us there are alternatives?

Corporations, Chemicals, and Health

This an an abridged version of an essay that appeared in More Voices From The Land.

by Bruce Carlson

Big Macs and Twinkies. Fast food and junk food as alternatives to well-rounded meals. Bovine growth hormone for more, not better, milk production from dairy cows. Steroids producing bigger, less fatty cattle and hogs quicker. Katsup as a vegetable in school lunch rooms.

To me one thing is clear: corporate America has only one priority: the bottom line, profits, and shareholders' dividends. These outweigh concerns for Americans' health and the health of the planet.

I spoke with a farmer who was participating in the University of Wisconsin's bovine growth hormone research. He belabored the point that the cows given the hormone got very thin, their hair lost its shine, their skin became scaly. He was impressed with the increased production, but he felt there would be no way he could put his prized herd through the anguish of altered health.

I realize this land grant college, in conjunction with Monsanto, is concerned about putting out a new biotechnology breakthrough that will bring in profits and prestige. In their desire for so-called progressive research, there seems to be no concern for the health of the dairy cows. My friend, who milks thirty to forty cows, could not justify this increased production because of the harm it was causing his animals. More important, he couldn't bear the thought of drinking milk from a sickly looking creature. Quality not quantity means a lot to him.

As the universities and our government push the control of food production from small farms to large and corporate farms, their indifference to the health of animals and the health of the soil that provides the animals' food, seems to signify a lack of concern for human health.

Farms that don't care about the health of a dairy cow are addicted to the profits that more production brings. Capitalism has created this monster that seems to have only its financial health as a concern.

I say enough is enough. If the government and powers that be will not protect our health and well being, it's up to us. We must demand food and water that are from a healthy source. We must make decisions daily that will effect a change in the way food is grown and distributed. We need to treat animals, soil, air, and water like the precious commodities they are. The stress on life that modern civilization has created can only be tolerated by nature for so long. Something will give. Let's change directions before it's too late.

BILL WELSH

In June 1991, when I was first looking for farmers for this project, especially farmers with an interest in land stewardship, Bruce Carlson recommended Bill Welsh, an organic farmer. In September I met Bill, Esther, and Greg on one of their farm tours. Bill, who bears a striking resemblance to Grant Wood, is a bespectacled, nearly stout man with a keen sense of humor, almost always dressed in bib overalls.

The Day the Welsh Family Farm Turned Around

Friday, May 10th, 1981, is a day that I will always remember. My day started at sunup. It was corn planting time in Iowa, which means long days in the fields. We started with chores at the home place and figured out how we could make the best use of the day. A bit of anxiety was pushing us because the following day, at noon, we were to leave for Dubuque to attend the college graduation ceremonies for our eldest son, Greg. We decided that I would start planting, while Gary went to the other farm, "Pat's," as it was called, to feed the cows.

I had just pulled into the field with the corn planter when I saw Gary racing to the field where I was working. I knew as soon as I saw him coming that something was very wrong. When he got to where I was, he jumped out of the pickup and hollered, "Come quick, the cows at Pat's are crazy!" We rushed to get over there, stopping at the house only long enough to call the vet.

As we arrived at Pat's, the first thing I saw was one cow lying dead. As I walked into the lot where the cows were, one of my favorite cows took after me and chased me over the fence. I remember thinking, what in the world is wrong with her! She was always such a gentle animal. Then we noticed three more dead cows piled on top of one another in the corner of the fence and the others running, as hard as they could, around the lot. Soon the vet arrived and he immediately said, "They are being poisoned by something."

A search began to find the source. We looked, we thought, and we looked some more. We found nothing. Soon four other veterinarians arrived to help. Brothers and neighbors were called to help, and in less than an hour the yard was full of cars. The search continued for a cause, but nothing was found.

The veterinarians decided we just had to start getting the cows into a catch chute so they could be injected with an antidote. Someone went to get the chute, others went after gates to make a runway to guide the cattle into the chute. At the same time, it was decided that one of the dead cows should be sent to a diagnostic lab. The nearest lab was contacted, and they said they would be glad to do the testing, but due to the fact that it was Friday, they could not get at it until Monday. Nevertheless, my brother Bernard was chosen for that task. Someone else went to get a manure loader to hoist the cow into the back of his pickup. Bernard immediately left for Madison, Wisconsin with a dead cow lying in the back of his pickup with all four feet in the air.

Bernard tells the story that when he got to Madison, he wasn't sure how to get to the laboratory. He saw two young men standing on the street corner, so decided to ask them for directions. As he approached them he decided it would be more fun to ask, "Where's the closest McDonald's?"

At Pat's, the job of putting the cows into the chute began. We were told that this would have to be done every four hours for at least forty-eight to seventy-two hours, maybe longer. Plans started developing on who was going to help with each succeeding shift so that we would have enough help to get through the night. The cows moved into the chute fairly easy the first trip, but each succeeding time it became more and more difficult, until at last, we were literally carrying some of them. Each time we put them through the chute, more had died.

Sometime in the afternoon, between "chute jobs," I was sitting on the fence, still trying to figure out what had happened. Then I remembered, there was a bale of hay that the cows were not eating. I had told Gary the day before that he should not give them more new hay until they had cleaned that bale up. I started wondering where that bale had come from and Gary remembered exactly, because there were very few bales left in the shed. We all went to the hay shed and soon found the problem. We found parts of a decomposed paper Dyfonate bag (an insecticide used for rootworm control) laying on the floor where that bale had been. Going back to the feeder where the refused hay bale was, we found parts of the same Dyfonate bag. The mystery was solved.

We continued to give the cows their antidote shots every four hours. Between each exhausting session, I felt very troubled about whether or not to try and go to Greg's graduation the following day. The decision was tearing my guts out. I had often dreamed about the day Greg would graduate from college, now would I even be able to go?

I spent the night in the barn, getting only a few minutes of sleep while lying on a bale of straw. This was probably the longest night of my life. By morning, the decision to go to graduation seemed much easier, probably because I was too tired to argue with my son, Gary, my brothers, and my neighbors, who had been telling me all along that they would take care of things.

At noon we left for Dubuque. I still wondered if I was doing the right thing. The time spent in Dubuque seems hazy. All I really remember was how proud I was of Greg for accomplishing something I had never been able to do.

When we returned home Sunday evening, I went straight to Pat's to check on the cows. By now thirteen had died. Soon the vet arrived again. They had decided at noon that day to discontinue the antidote shots because they really weren't sure if the last cows had died from the poison or from the antidote. The vet and I sat on the fence that evening and talked for a long time. He told me that a tablespoon of the insecticide, Dyfonate, spread evenly enough throughout the bale, could have killed all those cows and that if we used five pounds of it per acre for twenty years that we would have one hundred pounds of it somewhere in our environment. It might be dispersed, washed away by rains into nearby ponds, creeks, rivers, and eventually into the ocean, but it would always be somewhere. It is not biodegradable. It was in this discussion that I first realized that the chemicals we were using in farming were the same ones used in chemical warfare that I had learned about years before as an instructor in atomic, biological, and chemical warfare during my tour of duty in the Air Force. Frankly, that scared the hell out of me. I vowed that Sunday evening that never again would I use that product or anything like it on any land that I owned.

That is when the search for ways to farm without chemicals began. We didn't know where or how to start, but were convinced that we had to find a way. Planting time, 1982, became a real nightmare. We were unsure of what to plant where, or what to try first, but we were positively sure we would not use any more insecticide. Some of our crops that year were not that great, but we were learning and became confident we could do better next year.

The Way Back

by Greg Welsh

"Sometimes you have to go a long distance out of your way to come back a short distance correctly."

—Edward Albee

I grew up on a farm in northeast Iowa, the eldest son of eight children, nurtured by my father's pride and embraced by the land. But eventually everyone needs something of his own, a sense of who he is. Trying to find mine, I rejected a proud father and the vulnerable land, and I learned a lot about selfishness, anger, loneliness, before my search brought me back to where I started. I don't know if I'll ever find that elusive self I was after, but I may have found a crucial part of it in what I tried to leave behind.

My first eight years on the farm were magical. Each day brought with it its own adventure, the fascination at the birth of a calf, a new corner of the hay barn to explore in awe. And the crazy yearning, the consuming hunger to operate the machinery. I remember how my brother, Gary, and I planned for weeks the best way to ask Dad if we could drive the tractor in third gear. After a fairly extensive safety speech, he, miraculously, said yes. You've never seen two happier boys.

But few idylls last forever, and never those that begin when we're young. Third gear advanced to road gear, and I began a spiral of personal disillusion and dissatisfaction about the same time Earl Butz began in earnest his assault on the land and the American family farm. Expansion, yield, fencerow to fence-row production, "feed the world."

We rented more land, poured on fertilizer and pesticides, tried for that ultimate yield. Chores now were done with syringe in hand. Dead livestock no longer phased me at all. It seemed normal. The veterinarian almost lived with us. He sent us his bill as we buried the animals. We were farming by the book, and it was tearing our family apart.

It was a question both of "too much" and "too little." Too much productivity that meant too much work, too much debt, too much anger, with too little return, too little communication, too little time for love. I was old enough to know there was more than one right way, and I had ideas of my own. But my father didn't seem capable of listening. He only seemed capable of working hard. I hated him for working so stubbornly hard.

In contrast, town kids had it made. No chores to speak of. They could play baseball whenever they wanted. Often I would stay overnight with friends in town, but seldom asked friends to come to the farm. I told my mother they wouldn't have any fun. I was in high school, and I was ashamed of the farm, my family, my life.

I longed, vaguely but completely, to make a difference, and it seemed clear that I couldn't do so at home. So I dreamed of escape: to college, to law school, to a time when I could exist on my own terms, without the stigma of where I'd come from and who I'd been.

In college I got to be a town kid. I missed calving in the spring, the planting, the field work. I missed harvest. I would go back to the farm gladly on vacation. But the romance was short-lived each time, and I was equally glad to leave again. I never gave a thought to returning for good to the embrace the land held me in as a child.

While I was at college, nothing every really replaced my love for my family. But that love did take some curious turns. Naively, I pictured myself a successful lawyer with enough money to help them out of their mounting debt. I pictured them loving me finally for what I'd made of myself. I pictured myself recognized. But I never pictured myself sharing my life with them steadily, completely, as I had before and as many rural families still do.

As for my father, I felt sorry for him. Because he was still on the farm. Because he was still working hard. Because he still didn't know what I already was sure of.

My world expanded with each new possibility, each new friend, each new bit of knowledge I acquired, even as it shrank from the lack of intimacy with the people and things that formed my heart as I grew up. After a close college friend met my parents at graduation, he turned and said to me, "I didn't know you came from a farm." Somehow I'd forgotten to tell him. Somehow I'd forgotten.

Then, in the spring of 1981, an incident occurred which I see now as the beginning of my gradual return to the love of both my father and the land, love I had always needed and will never outgrow. A year earlier, at planting time, an empty bag of Dyfonate insecticide had been overlooked and left on the floor of our hay shed. A little later, the shed was filled with large, round bales of hay, which during the year we fed to our cattle.

Now, after a whole year, the bale of hay that had been on top of the empty Dyfonate bag had absorbed enough residual pesticide to poison forty full-grown pregnant cows. Thirteen eventually died. It didn't take a college education to realize there was something incredibly wrong with what had happened. I was outraged. Why were we permitted to buy such toxic products? Why were they allowed to be on the market in the first place? And what about the six to ten pounds per acre of Dyfonate that we and a large percentage of farmers like us used each year to control rootworms? What had it already done, what was it still doing, to our soil, our water, our food, ourselves?

The experience shattered my father's rigid views of farming. He swore he'd never use chemicals again. He found a reason to fight, to believe, a reason for more than stubborn work. He opened, grew, rediscovered discovery. He became approachable. I saw that he could see me, hear me again. I saw there could be a way.

But I wasn't ready. For four years I had pursued other dreams, had tested other environments, and they weren't so easily abandoned. I spent the winter working in Corpus Christi, Texas. I kept in touch with my professors, applied to law schools. I knew what I wanted.

In Texas I developed a condition I convinced myself was cancer. And why not cancer? Look at what the Dyfonate had done to our cattle. I remembered how, in high school, the daughter of a neighboring farmer was diagnosed with cancer. Cancer seemed to me the logical, horrifying inheritance of farm families, the deadly bequest of chemical agriculture.

Suddenly my life seemed so very short, my accomplishments so very few. I'd made no difference, I would never make a difference. I was angry, frightened, lonely. I was dying.

I went home.

It took about two months for the official verdict to come in. Expecting the worst, I cried all the way to the doctor. But I did not have cancer. I had a serious infection, but it could be cured completely and fairly quickly with antibiotics. I had gotten a stay of execution. The relief was amazing. So was the feeling of stupidity. My imagination surprised me.

Nothing really changed. And everything did. If my cancer wasn't real, the threat of cancer to myself, my family, my neighbors still was. The economics of overproductive agribusiness threatened a whole way of life, my way of life, despite the years I tried to deny it. And the chemical dependency at the heart of that economics threatened not only the lives of farm families, but of anyone eating the food farms produced, or drinking water from contaminated aquifers.

I, too, rediscovered discovery.

Of course transformations are never really instantaneous. After every turning point there are residues left of our former selves that only patience can eradicate. For awhile I became a self-righteous environmentalist, the most righteous environmentalist in the county for sure. I was intolerant of the sheer blockheadedness of many farmers in the light of my new found truth. There were still heated arguments with my father, despite our similar views.

It was clear to me that the natural, organic life of the soil was a slow, dynamic process never to be completed. But it took much longer for me to see that the inner lives of men and women, my father's and my own included, are similar processes.

It seems to me now the true quality of both the soil and the spirit, of all life, should not be judged on what it is at any given moment, like a finished product, but should be loved for the emergent things they are. It seems to me now that all things are continually making themselves and each other. And there seems little need for amends. Everything—the crops, the laughter in my father's eyes—is reconciliation.

I am always amazed at the amount of life in the soil, at the resiliency of it, and I am convinced we should do nothing to destroy its creative ability. And I am amazed, too, at the life, love, and resiliency in my father's heart and, to my surprise, in my own. I'm amazed and afraid, and I pray I will soon cease doing anything that might endanger that creativity.

Part V:

SMALL TOWNS

Of this group of twelve stories, the first six came from the Clermont, Iowa workshop. They portray our collective image, accounts or not, of small towns logn ago. We begin with them.

KHAKI NELSON

Khaki's given name is "Gladys," but no one ever calls her that. Khaki and her husband, William, farmed and sold Pioneer seeds in the Clermont area for thirty years.

Saturday Nights in Clermont

The sound of water pumping and the smell of a kerosene stove heating up. A large copper boiler is filled with water and put to heat on the stove. Mom and Dad lift the heated water into a round, galvanized tub. I stand back, watch and wonder how soon before I'm stripped of clothing and dunked in the tub. Lowered into the water, I shut my eyes tight as soap suds trickle over my head, down my face and body. I take a deep breath, hoping it's store soap and not homemade lye soap. I'm scrubbed to a shine, big sis is next. I scamper into my clothes— a pretty, starched print dress and patent leather shoes.

I shake my blond hair to get it dry, thinking, "I wish I was a teenager like my sis, with dark hair and beautiful." Mom and Dad are pretty fancy in their Saturday night attire. A change from Dad's bib overalls and Mom's feed sack dress and apron. I hop up and down singing, "Let's go to Clermont, I want to go to Clermont!"

The family scampers into the car and sighs with relief as the car starts and the four tires are full of air, at that moment there's a rumble of thunder and a big black cloud appears in the west. "Wait," my dad says, "if it's going to storm we can't start out. We have five miles to go and the road may get muddy." We file out of the car with heads hanging low, put our good clothes away, and wait for next Saturday night.

A week passes, same routine, a beautiful night, stars shining. We bounce down the road in the old car, anxious to see friends in town. The dolls, Shirley and Alice, are seated beside me, they will enjoy a night in town.

The lights show up distinctly as we near town and drive over the rumbly, rattly bridge. Clermont is alive and buzzing. Cars are everywhere, and streets are lined with people. What a sight! Oh, so exciting!

Dad says, "Hope we can find a place to park." The band is playing a peppy tune, and we immediately begin keeping time with our hands and feet to the beat of the drums and the wonderful brass horns. The aroma of freshly popped corn floats through the air from Nora Halverson's popcorn stand. Five cents for a nice, big sack with plenty of real melted butter. The stores are all open for business, three grocery stores to choose from. Tonight we get the week's supplies. We enter the grocery store, which seems so large and well stocked. I trail along behind my mom, hoping the storekeeper will notice me. Sometimes they give candy treats to the kids. Mom has a list of things she needs, tells the clerk, and proceeds to run here and there to gather up the things and bring them to the counter. She seems to know where everything is, and in a few minutes has it all together and sacked. We have sugar, yeast, oatmeal, raisins, flour (a very large sack), and wieners (they are hooked together and look like a chain of beads). The money received from selling the eggs down the street at the produce store will more than cover the bill. We are lucky we don't have to buy meat, milk, butter, lard, canned vegetables, or fruit. We have those things on the farm. We take the groceries to the car, and Mom meets with other ladies in front of Lubke's (five and dime). They visit about the week's happenings, upcoming marriages, and new babies born. With several aunts, cousins, and other relatives there it seems like a weekly family reunion.

The men congregate down the street at Pringle's, Gerner's, or the John Deere shop. The talk gets pretty lively, and sometimes heated about politics, crops, and prices. There is a barber shop near the John Deere shop with a neat red and white barber pole. The fellows think Saturday a good time for a haircut and some good conversation.

Meanwhile we kids gather around the water fountain on the corner by the grocery store. The boys get pretty wild with the water and splash it at ts. We giggle, laugh, and shout at the boys, "We'll tell on you." We enjoy strolling up and down the street. On one side the band is playing, across from the telephone office and Crowe's Drug Store. There is also romance in the air for the teenagers. A boy that's sweet on my sister brings her a box of cherry centers almost every Saturday night. I tease her, but she still shares those yummy chocolates with me.

A free movie is held several times during the summer. This is a very special treat, for we rarely go to a movie theater. It is set up outdoors between the old bank building and Gerner's. We sit on planks held up on nail kegs. My favorite movie is "The Little Rascals" with Spanky and Alfalfa.

After a great evening, Mom and Dad say, "It's time to go home. To-

morrow is Sunday, and we will be coming back to Clermont for church."
Before going home sometimes we go to Peck's Ice Cream parlor for a treat,
or better still, we take home a quart of ice cream and eat it before it melts.
    Sleep comes over me driving home, but as we make the turn into the
driveway our trusty watch dog barks and wakes me with a start. Sleepy as
I am I won't miss out on eating that great tasting ice cream.

DORIS MARTIN

*A retired school teacher, Doris keeps active with all kinds of volunteer projects.
She was a driving force in the writers workshop in Clermont.*

Brick City Ice Cream

My parents and I moved to Elgin the
summer of 1930 before my second birthday. My brothers Bob and Jack
were born in 1930 and 1932. This was after the Depression, so money was
very scarce, although I wasn't aware of that. I believe that children who are
loved, fed, and cared for don't realize how poor their families may be.
    We had no close relatives in the area, and my parents made friends
slowly. My dad worked six days a week as a farmer, so he wanted to stay
home on Sunday. My brothers and I played long, involved games that
lasted for days, so we wanted to stay home too. My mother couldn't drive.
She was always home working. Occasionally on Sunday after church Mom
would say, "Let's go for a ride." First she had to convince Dad, then get us
away from our play. She would sweeten the offer with, "We'll stop in Brick
City to get ice cream cones." That got our attention, we got very little ice
cream.
    The four mile ride to Brick City was long and boring but we were
thrilled when we got there. We knew where it got its name—all those brick
stores on Main Street and the brick homes around town.
    We would park near Pringle's and Dad would go in. Jack was in front
with Mom, Bob and I in the back. We would sit at the same side window to
watch Dad go. It never occurred to us we might go in too.
    Finally Dad would return with one of those pressed cardboard contain-
ers with five vanilla cones that probably cost a nickel apiece. We would sit
in the car and eat those delicious treats.
    Years later when I heard the name Clermont for the town my first reac-

tion was, "No, that's Brick City, our ice cream town." Today I live in one of those brick houses, I walk to the Gas and Goods for delicious ice cream that costs fifty cents a dip. However, I don't think I have ever had ice cream that tasted better than those cones in that old car with my family.

LAVERNE SWENSON

LaVerne Swenson's family has a rich history in Clermont. He, his wife Grace, and their children farm.

Saturday Nights

When Saturday night came we really looked forward to hearing something different and seeing something other than the mouth of a horse and the rear of a cow, the "udder" end. Movies were shown where the post office now stands, and later in the opera house. They cost a dime. We always got the news first, mostly war news.

In the early fifties we had outdoor band concerts. Cars would park around the blocks where the post office now stands, and people would sit in the cars and listen to the concerts. They didn't parallel park, but parked diagonally, so more cars could park close to the concert. After every song they'd blow their horns. The better the song, the more they blew. After the concert we'd get paid three pieces of paper. They each said five cents on them. Fifteen cents a concert, to be spent in town.

Really, the best Saturday nights came when I started enjoying the girl of my dreams. The band concerts lasted about an hour, and the folks liked to visit afterwards. I didn't have a car, so I'd have to hurry for maybe an hour visit with Grace. If luck was with us, we'd get to double date with someone who had a car. That was the beginning of our life forever together.

MIKE FINNEGAN

Since moving to town after retiring from farming, Mike is active in anything that promotes Clermont, and has received the Governor's Award for his efforts. The following is an excerpt from "My Early Memories of Clermont."

Burkard Riegel

Burkard Riegel is a legend. I remember well when I started farming in the late fifties. Riegel did many repair jobs for me, and if there wasn't a clear plan or method on the tip of his tongue, he would say, "Let me think about it!"

Everyone was always amazed at Burkard's method of bookkeeping. His system was immediate and accurate. He would often charge for his services with what seemed to me very little hesitation, anything from a nickel for a small job to a dollar for a big job.

Dad would ask, "How much today, Riegel?"

"Oh, gimme thirty-five cents."

Dad would hand him a dollar, and Burkard's hands would go into action, the quarter in one pocket, nickels and dimes in another. His bib overalls held the bills. Never examining or eyeballing the change, he would complete the transaction fast, and we would be on our way.

Burkard never liked to be bothered when he was busy at something, and he worked very early in the morning and late at night when farmers didn't come in to bother him. If he was deeply taken up with his work he often refused to look up when a farmer walked in to pick up his fixed piece. The finished jobs would be neatly stacked against the right wall as you walked in, and Burkard would quickly look up and nod in the direction of your fixed piece, and you were on your way knowing your bill was scribbled on some sort of crude but accurate account record.

LOIS AMUNDSON

Lois grew up near Elgin and moved to Clermont after marrying her husband, Roger. They farmed east of Clermont until moving to town several years ago.

Party Line

Moving to Clermont as a shy young bride in 1955 brought many new experiences, one of them the old central telephone system and local operators. Having grown up in a neighboring community where we had converted to the dial telephone when I was six years old, this was a new experience. I learned to use the telephone by simply dialing the numbers I needed to reach friends or relatives.

Several days after moving into the old farmhouse, I happened to see my mother-in-law. She said she had been trying to reach me by telephone, but that I hadn't answered. Sure, I had heard the telephone ring many times, but we were on a big party line with eleven families and eleven different rings coming into the house. I couldn't differentiate three longs and one short (our ring) from three short or three long or one short and two long. As time went by I finally learned which ring was ours and answered the phone.

To make a call was also quite a challenge. It took perseverance. First you picked up the receiver and listened to hear if any one of the other families was using the phone, and quite often they were, so you waited. Next you gave the crank a ring to signal the operator you wanted to make a call. If the operator was busy with another call, you waited. If the party you were trying to call was already using the phone and the line was busy, you waited, and probably tried later. It took a lot of patience and endurance to accept this phone system.

Our particular phone had an extra button that had to be pushed and released before you could talk. If one of the neighbors was already using the phone, you could pick up the receiver and listen, and not release the button, and the neighbors couldn't tell you were listening, or "rubbering," as it was called. The extra button was not very common, but rubbering was. Of course, no one admitted they rubbered, but if there was any news in the neighborhood, it seemed that everyone knew it right away.

Calling a girlfriend for a date was a real trial for a young man. If he used his home phone, the whole community knew who the girl was, where they were going, etc. Worse yet, if the girl turned him down for the date, they knew the young man had been rejected and humiliated. So many a young gentleman made a trip to town and used the phone at the central office to do his wooing.

One fear or concern people had in using the party line was that the neighbors or the operators were listening so they chose their words very carefully, trying to get a message across, but not mentioning the specific topic. When a friend called she chatted a little before she asked me how the item that she had sent home with my husband had worked out. I was perplexed, I didn't remember any package or gift that Roger had brought home for me. I said I was sorry, but that I couldn't think of what he had brought home. I was not used to the guessing game yet. Really, I was very embarrassed, as someone had given me a gift, and I was so ungrateful that I couldn't remember what it was. She went on, describing it as long and part of that other gift. I was still blank. Finally the conversation ended, and she said she would tell me when she saw me.

As soon as Roger got home, I asked what gift or package he had brought the other day. He went over to the back of the truck and pulled out the handle to a dust mop. I had received a dust mop as a bridal gift, but as the handle was long and would have been hard to gift wrap, she waited and sent it over later. This was another tradition that I had to learn to accept.

I always smile when I remember Roger's grandmother, a very nice, older Norwegian lady. She figured she had out-foxed those telephone operators by always speaking Norwegian when she talked on the telephone to friends and relatives. I suppose she never gave it a thought that the operator might have been Norwegian too.

Eventually many communities got the dial telephone, eliminating the local operators. About 1965, the Clermont area got the dial system, but we still had eight families on our line. A great joy for me came later, in 1973, when we received our own private dial telephone, but I still find myself picking up the receiver and listening before I dial to hear if anyone is talking.

JENNIFER OLUFSEN

Jennifer, an accountant, is a newcomer to Clermont, and her neighbors are glad she chose to move there. Her daughter Chantel, who contributed to Clermont, Iowa, *is in elementary school.*

Moving from the City to Clermont in 1992

The clock strides five, time to pick up my six-year-old daughter and head off to Clermont, Iowa. We have been driving up to northeast Iowa every other weekend, hoping to relocate to Clermont. There are so many hurdles. It is yet another move, but for right now I just want to get on the road and not worry about all the problems. I drive past the crack house on the corner, and past the sign that marks the "Drug Free Zone," and it strengthens my resolve to make this move to Clermont work somehow!

It is starting to snow as we get on the interstate. The driving conditions are getting worse, but I have the same feeling that I used to have coming home from college at Christmas. Four long hours later, when we finally top the ridge overlooking the valley, it looks like a Christmas card. I have the feeling that we are coming home.

"Where is Clermont, and why do you want to move there?" my city friends asked. It is hard to describe. It is wanting a warm feeling of peace and security and belonging for my daughter, a sense of belonging and roots.

We came up for the first time for Threshing Days. Vernon Oakland had called me and asked if my daughter would like to ride on his threshing machine with his six-year-old son Kevin. I was going to have a table at the craft show, so I was busy while the parade was setting up. "Where is Chantel Marie?" I looked left and right and finally straight up. It is probably a good idea that I did not know what the threshing machine looked like ahead of time. At the end of the parade, Vernon set Kevin and Chantel off on the main street downtown. My husband was supposed to keep track of her. He came back and asked, "Have you seen Chantel?" I was frantic. (Relax, this Clermont!") She had met up with Jeff Guyer, and he had taken her to Valhalla for a soda. That is why we live here. ("Relax. This is Clermont!!")

The pastor's wife—Clermont's unofficial welcome wagon hostess—said, "Welcome home" to us at church, as if we had only been away on a journey. The church, a different denomination than I had been attending, was filled with warm and friendly people and opened the doors to all who came through.

The K-12 school has modern facilities but still has a country school feel about it. Some of the teachers are going on their third generation of students.

My daughter always wakes up early in Clermont, although we often came in after 11:00 P.M. the night before. She woke up to the strange noises of birds and snowy quiet instead of sirens and traffic. "Mom, can I go outside?" It occurs to me that she is probably the only six year old in town whose mother thinks that she needs to be chaperoned to go outside. When we later moved here, it would take one full year to let her go alone to the barn, which is within eyesight of the house. The neighbors must have thought I was far too overprotective.

People greet us on the streets. My daughter has learned not to talk to strangers in the city, but this was so much nicer.

My daughter did a one and a half gainer off the swing set at school and needed to have her head sewn up. The school secretary called me at work, one hour away, and managed so well to tell me calmly that I had to come home. A good friend and very experienced Mom had picked her up and taken her to the local doctor. In the city I worked at a big hospital with the most updated equipment, and here the country doctor was going to sew her face up in his office! He was great. Gentle and calming, with hands as steady as a rock, he sewed up her forehead. For the next couple of weeks people whose names I could not always remember, came up to me and asked, "How is our girl?"

I have lived on three continents and in six different states. I did not move my family here because we were born here or because this is where the job is. We chose this town and are thankful for the privilege of living here. Clermontians are warm, caring, real people. They respect the work ethic and enjoy life with gusto. We live in a wonderful neighborhood. People here help each other out, and when you receive such good help, you look forward to pitching in and helping when you can. What a great place to live!

104

JERRY KELLY

Jerry lives in Clermont with his wife and three children. He is in the building supply business, and wants to be just like his dad when he grows up.

A Changing Neighborhood

Where do all these people driving down U.S. 18 come from? Where are they headed? Have they passed through out little town before, or will they come again? Think back to the last trip you took through towns large and small, towns that you had never seen before. What were the impressions that stayed with you, and why? Think about it. Rewind that video tape in your mind and pay closer attention this time. Why can one village stand out so much clearer in your mind than all those other nameless, faceless ones? And which do you suppose our dear Clermont is to most of those passing through in that constant, never-ending parade called U.S. 18?

Walk through St. Peter's cemetery and you'll see names on the weathered, crumbling tombstones that you won't find in Clermont's current phone book. Some family trees have run out of branches, or have been transplanted to more fertile ground, or to climates more to their liking. The dates on those monuments start with 1800-something, and list birth places in foreign continents. Those people came to this valley with hopes and dreams, visions of the future for themselves and their families. Do you suppose they saw any come true? We hope so, but in most cases we'll never know.

Wouldn't it be neat to be able to look back once into the eyes of some of those forgotten people who called Clermont home? Do you suppose their eyes carried the same sparkle that some of the kids on the streets have today? Do you suppose the young fathers of today go to the bank and tell stories of their hopes and dreams, with the same conviction, the same determination, the same lust that these nameless, forgotten brothers did, fifty, sixty, seventy-five years ago? I bet they do!

I don't share the opinion that these are the worst times in fifty years. Doom and gloom has been with us since Cain and Abel. And we just keep going, don't we? I think that no matter how bad things might seem, in twenty years these will be the good old days. In a few more years, the names on the stones will be worn away by the weather, and some think there won't even be anyone left to care or disagree. And the reason I disagree is very simple.

The next generation of people who migrate and settle here are the ones driving through town on U.S. 18 today. They won't be coming on a boat from some distant shore to flee famine or persecution. They are, this minute, drifting on the sea of uncertainty, in a ship called discontent. As long as we keep the light on in our lighthouse they will find us. I can give a very simple reason for my theory. There are some names in our phone book that weren't there twenty years ago. Times they are a-changing. The next time you are on Highway 18, wave at the drivers of the cars you meet. One of them might be your new neighbor.

The next two stories first appeared in Independence, Iowa. *The experiences they recount are not confined to small towns, but are included for the quality of their writing.*

DELORES MARTIN

Delores was part of the Independence, Iowa workshop. She is in sales, but her real passion in life is writing. She enjoys reading and crafts in her spare time.

The Flood of 1990

I looked out the upstairs window one more time at the bend in the Wapsipinicon River, a scant block away. All morning, this late August day in 1990, I had been monitoring its rise. Landmark after landmark slowly succumbed to the insidiously creeping water.

My house was beside the old Greenley Flour Mill, parallel with the dam, with nothing between it and the water except Veteran's Park. A flood was forecast, so here I was again running upstairs to get a good view and checking the river's impending rise.

This time, about 10:30 in the morning, the water was starting to trickle over the high bank and run down the street and through the park. My heart thudded in my chest. I had never seen the water this high. I looked again to make sure I was not imagining it. As I looked again it gained stature and looked as though a wall of water was heading straight for my house.

I rushed downstairs to tell my husband we had to get the cars out of the yard. We had my son's '65 Dodge and my cousin's '38 Chevy in the backyard, and of course no battery in either one at this time. My husband just looked up and said, "Don't get excited, there's plenty of time." After all, the intersection filled up with water and came up almost to our backyard every time we had a flood or a heavy rain, but never had reached the house, not even in the flood of '68.

I ran upstairs again and looked. This time it was a solid sheet of water pouring over the park, resembling the Mississippi rather than the Wapsi. I frantically ran back to my husband, urging him to hurry.

"It's coming up fast, we've got to move!" I screeched, sounding like a Blue Jay. "Everything is going under water!"

About ten minutes later he finally went out to see for himself. By then the water was ankle deep throughout our yard. We didn't have a chain to pull the cars, and by the time he went to call about borrowing one to move the cars, the water was waist deep, and it was useless. There was no way to get anything close enough to pull them out.

At that point we rushed to the basement to check on it. As we descended the stairs we heard the ominous sound of splashing, trickling water. This is okay out in the woods somewhere but has no business coming from my basement.

My basement is about one hundred years old and formed of limestone rocks stacked upon one another. The water level in the yard was so high that the water was seeping around the stones and creating miniature waterfalls in the basement.

The two of us formed a box brigade to start throwing things out of the basement. He was wading around grabbing boxes and throwing them up to me, as I stood halfway up the basement stairs. I then flung them out the basement door onto the lawn.

A very few minutes later the water was up to my husband's knees. I yelled at him, "Get out now, you'll be electrocuted!" I couldn't remember how high the furnace controls were, but I knew they were the lowest point at which water would make contact with electricity.

The water in the yard and basement had a different feel to it from the normal river water. Maybe it was just because it had invaded my domain, but it seemed slimy on my feet and legs. My hands slipped on the wet boxes my husband threw at me. The world had a dank, musty smell that had not been in my neighborhood before.

I looked at the furnace and then at the breaker box on the wall. "Oh my God!" I breathed. The water was going to cover the breaker box. I rushed up the stairs again and tried to look up the number of the light company. I knew we had to get the electricity shut off. Finally I called and had them shut off our service.

We left the rest of the stuff we owned in the basement as it started to float around like multicolored fishing bobbers, and looked out at the water-soaked world. We could no longer see any of the park, only the tops of the speed limit signs. Our neighborhood, our street, our yard were all a dark rolling mass of water. Even the huge cannon in the park had disappeared under a sheet of fast moving water.

We ran next door to the mill to check what was happening below the dam. I had never seen anything like it. The deafening sound of rushing water had entirely engulfed the dam, there was little to tell that it existed.

My adrenaline was pumping so fast I was almost giddy. There was nothing at all I could do. I was, for the first time in my life, entirely help-less. I watched the water creep up. It was now around three sides of my house.

Every few minutes I would run to the basement steps to see if it was going to come into the main floor of the house. I was like a barefoot bather walking onto a sun drenched beach on a first summer outing.

Now I had no lights and no radio or TV to get the current news. Was the river really still rising? It couldn't be, but the marks I had picked out on the street proved it was still going up.

We could not even decently clean up at home. The water heater as well as the washer, dryer, and furnace, all in the basement, were destroyed.

Night finally fell but there was no peacefulness to this sunset. The Main Street bridge had been closed because the water was still rising and roaring all about us. There was an unbelievable stream of onlookers and sightseers.

I was too frightened to even go in my house and rest. I passed through it to check the level of the water at each door, but could not relax with all that water gurgling beneath my feet in the basement.

The weather in late August here in Iowa can be horrid. I remember it was hot, and we didn't have a refrigerator to get a cool drink. I sat on my front porch in a sort of daze. I did not feel safe in my own house.

I kept imagining that if the water came around the fourth side of my house that meant it was over the main street and most of Independence would be inundated.

By Saturday evening and Sunday, I think half of Waterloo was driving slowly around our town looking at all the damage.

We who lived here, or rather, at this time survived here, could do noth-ing.

In the aftermath of the flood, life did not immediately get back to normal. Slowly, inch by painstaking inch, the waters receded. One day the river was back within its prescribed banks and the sump pump was furiously working in the basement.

As the waters receded down our street they left in their wake a slimy, smelly mass of mud and thousands of dead night crawlers. One day in the hot sun and the muck and dead worms wafted a very unappetizing aroma over the area.

In the park behind my house, the picnic tables were gone, as well as two of the bench seats that were cemented in along the river's edge.

As the sump pump finished its job, the heartbreaking work began. Every single thing that had been stored in the basement had to be carried out to the curb to be disposed of. I had a veritable mountain there awaiting the sanitation trucks.

My heart was heavy as I carried piles of leatherwork patterns and magazines to the curb. When I found a snapshot of my grandson as a baby that had been in my workshop, I sat down in the mud and cried. I knew what it had been, but the colors had run and streaked, so it was barely recognizable.

My husband got angry. "It's only a picture," he stormed.

"I know," I lamented, "but it reminds me of all things I can't replace."

After removing our belongings and carrying up the heavy, soaked, dripping carpets, we had the back-breaking job of shoveling up inches of mud into five-gallon buckets and carrying them out. It was a hot, heavy, stinking, sweating, seemingly never-ending job.

While this work was going on we were fed twice a day by the Red Cross truck, which came by till we got our electricity restored. It was something I never thought I would be doing, but I was very thankful for something hot to eat.

We added more water to the basement and hosed off the walls and floor. Then we disinfected all the surfaces.

The flood was not really over for me until I got my new furnace installed at the end of November. It was getting very cold, and we were thankful for it. Until then my kerosene had only kept us grudgingly warm.

To this day I still get very nervous when the weatherman advises we are in a flash flood watch.

HANNAH CHESMORE

Hannah is a senior at Independence High School and works at the Dairy Queen. She is a member of student council.

$4.65

I have worked at Dairy Queen for one year and four months. I plan to work there throughout my high school career. When I applied at Dairy Queen, many of my casual acquaintances worked there. Since being hired, most of these acquaintances have become close friends.

When I lived in a small town, Rowley, just outside of Independence, going to Dairy Queen was a rare treat. Often my mom, my aunt Paula, and I would put on our pajamas and drive to Dairy Queen for a treat. I always got the same thing, a cherry dip cone. It amazed me. Why didn't the Dairy Queen fall off into the dip? I now know, from experience, that occasionally the Dairy Queen does fall into the dip.

Like all jobs, working at the DQ does get overbearing, but I don't complain too much. There's rarely a dull moment. Crying babies, cranky, worn-out mothers, picky ladies, people hard of hearing, little kids who can't make up their minds, the list goes on and on.

There's one man who comes through the DQ drive-through quite often. For awhile he always ordered a small vanilla shake. Just recently he changed his order to a small root beer.

"Hi. Welcome to Dairy Queen. May I help you?" I asked very routinely.

"Just a minute!" the man replied quickly.

"Go ahead and order whenever you're ready."

Then I waited for what seemed an eternity.

"Are you still there?" the man asked very rudely.

"Yes, are you ready to order?" I asked very pleasantly and politely.

"I want a small beer," he ordered.

"That was a small root beer? Will that be all?"

There was no answer.

"Thank you, please proceed to the window."

It never fails. He always has to be the smart guy. He has to make it tough on all of us. A small beer, we all thought that was pretty funny. When he approaches the window nobody wants to collect the money from

110

him. He'll either complain about how much it costs or he'll make a pass at us. Hardly a turn on. Several times he has asked girls to marry him. However, I don't believe anyone has ever accepted. Sometimes I think minimum wage is good for a person my age, but on days like this a raise would be greatly appreciated.

It was the Fourth of July. The fireworks, which take place at the Mental Health Institute, had just gotten over. We had been swamped all night. However, after the fireworks it is always twice as busy. I was on drive-through with a friend of mine. The cars were backed up all the way through the DQ parking lot. We were mixing shakes and blizzards like mad. We always tried to be polite to the customers, but occasionally we slipped; they were usually understanding, *usually!*

One man came through and ordered two kid cones. He wanted us to give him cups to put his cones in. We politely explained to him that we weren't allowed to give out cups. He told us that was crazy, and that if we would just give him the cups he wouldn't tell. Like it mattered to us if he told anyone or not. We once again politely explained to him that we weren't able to do that. Then he started to get huffy and rude. Finally my friend went and got the man his cups. There were cars backed up, and we didn't have time to argue with him. She wasn't real pleasant when she gave him the cups. Big mistake! He threw a fit! He cussed and cussed at her. "You little smart *^*. Who the hell do you think you are?"

He wanted to know her name. He kept rambling on and on. We just shut the window and let him yell. He said he was going to call the owner. My friend cried. We all felt really bad for her. She didn't do anything wrong. Like I said before, sometimes minimum wage just isn't enough.

The Death of Innocence

by Barb Leppert

Where have our innocent children gone?

I have been teaching for almost thirty years, and until the last few years, have enjoyed it thoroughly. I delight in seeing children's eyes light up when they finally master a difficult concept, or in listening to their English assignments when they have been given a story to write. Their imaginations used to run wild and their stories were full of the fantasies of childhood.

A few years ago, the other fourth grade teacher and I noticed the change in the calibre of their work and the theme running through every writing assignment. We had to say finally, "No blood and guts stories," because all we were getting were Freddy Kruger stories.

The children of parents who were on drugs were finally showing up in our classrooms. Their attention span is about sixty seconds, they can't sit still, and some can't even stay in their seats long enough to complete an assignment. Their work is poor quality, and they don't care if it is.

They know more about vulgar sex acts and porno than I've ever heard of. Today a little girl came up and tattled that the boys were singing a song to the girls:

"Boys go to Mars for candy bars
Girls go to Venus to get some penis."

The week before we let out for Christmas vacation, we did some special projects. In art class we made a Christmas mouse with a candy cane in it. I asked them not to eat the candy canes until their moms and dads could see them. To keep them from eating them, I broke up the extra candy canes and gave them each a piece. One little girl sucked hers until the red was gone and the white had little holes in it. She held it up to the other kids and said, "Look guys, mine looks just like cocaine."

When we have five minutes before we go to a special class or to lunch, I let them go to the front of the room and tell a joke or a riddle, to get them used to speaking in front of a group. One student said, "I don't know any clean ones. Can we tell dirty ones?"

A few years ago at a teachers' meeting , a second grade teacher told of a little girl bringing her Teddy bear to school. At recess she put it on her desk and jumped on it. "I'm having sex with my Teddy bear," she laughed.

Second grade! Those children are only seven years old! What will the next generation of children be like, I wonder?

Declining Business

Anonymous

The following piece is an excerpt from an interview conducted with a small town merchant who wished to remain anonymous. While there is nothing in what he said that could be construed as critical of his town, still, in small towns people do not want to stand out.

I don't think people had a lot of money (in the early fifties), but on Friday and Saturday nights the town was just packed; everybody came to town. A kid could come to town with fifty cents or less and he could see a movie for ten cents and he could get a bag of popcorn or a coke, which would take care of maybe another quarter or twenty cents, and he had a pretty good time.

And the folks: Ma used to do her shopping at night and Dad would go down to the tavern closest to the grocery store and he'd sit and have a few beers while Mom was shopping. When the kids got out of the movie they'd all meet in the bar or in front of the bar to get Pa and off they'd go home.

There were just a lot of people all over the streets on Saturday nights. It was just a great time. The kids looked forward to coming to town, Mom did too. Pa did too. Of course he might've been in town during the week getting parts for his machinery and things like that.

That was the big night for the farmers. Of course people who worked the businesses, they all got paid probably on Friday, so their families had money, too, to spend. Then you only had one automobile; the farmer only had one automobile. Today everyone in the family has an automobile. Eighteen year olds, they've got to have a car. The missus has a car, Dad has a pickup truck.

With the advent of vehicles, people drive to a bigger shopping center, like La Crosse or Prairie du Chien or Cedar Rapids, a bigger area where there's more variety of stores. They always know what they can get in town, but they look for something a little different out of town. So they'll go to the malls now where there's ten shoe stores, twenty ladies' stores, and five men's stores, plus the knickknacks and the crafts and all that.

Well, the small town businessman, of course, he can't compete with a Wal-Mart or a K-Mart and places like that. I feel the quality, seventy percent of the time, is better here with our local merchants than at a K-Mart or Wal-Mart.

I don't go to them (out-of-town stores), unless I can't find it here, unless the price is way out of line here from what I can buy somewhere else. If it (the price) is close I always buy locally.

Even though back in the fifties it didn't seem like people had money, they supported all those stores that were here, where now I think the margin of profit has gone down in all local businesses. And if more people would stay in the community and shop, the businesses would do better and therefore that's reinvestment in the community, because most businesses that are in town will reinvest in the community, according to their profit margins.

As for the young people, there's nothing to keep them here. Say in the farming community, their fathers expect them to take over, but their children don't want the debt that the fathers accumulated over the years. And therefore they go on to bigger cities and try to find something else. There's just nothing here to keep them. The businesses, say, the merchants in the downtown area, their children don't seem overly happy with doing the same thing Ma and Dad did for forty years or whatever. They want to go out like any young person and see what the rest of the world's like. And a small community, like this, what will keep young people here? We don't know, and I'm sure studies have been done by somebody. I just don't know what would keep them here.

The Down Side

Anonymous

While this speaker was willing to be mentioned by name, I chose to omit it. The portrait of the town presented here is accurate and is true, in varying degrees, of other small towns. Clermont, however, seems a special place.

Q. You're hanging in here despite difficulties, so for you there are obviously good things here.

A. I made a choice to come back here, and I'm not even sure why. A combination of things. The environment. My family being here. There's also a comfortableness in small town living where you can really feel that you're a part of the community. People know you, they wave at you, and you walk down the street and people talk to you. My kids can go into the bakery, they can go to the store. They have a lot more freedom here, which is nice.

There are a lot of difficulties though, particularly in making a living.

It's not as expensive to live here as in a lot of places, but finding a way to make enough and being able to use any talents and abilities is a very difficult thing. You almost have to find your own way.

Q. Tell me about the difficulties some of the people have finding work around here.

A. Mostly what's available is your basic seven to three-thirty, a half an hour for lunch. You're chained to the treadmill, so to speak. They make minimum wage. I think the average wage here is probably five dollars an hour. I don't think it goes much higher, which makes it hard. People don't have enough money. It's always a struggle, you're always concerned about money.

Q. In your lifetime has the population held? Increased? Decreased? Do you have the same number of businesses?

A. I know the population has declined consistently since the town's heyday in the early 1900s. It has gone down continually. You see a lot of businesses come and go. People start a business, they try to hang in there for a while, ultimately they aren't able to keep it going. Most of the businesses that have been here are generational, have come down through the families and have been here awhile.

There's a lot of empty store fronts. You see a new store in one summer; the next summer, the following winter, someone else is in there. Again, the owners struggle, they work a lot of hours, those who make a go of it. They're really hitting it hard.

Q. Talk about the flight of the young, the high school graduates.

A. High school graduates can't wait to get out of town, most of them, particularly the ones who are bright and curious about the world. They have to get out of here, which in itself is very good. Living in a small town you can be sheltered from some of the things that are going on in the rest of the world, and I think it's important that our young people get out there and know the realities a little bit more. But most of them are not able to come back because of the job situation. Most of them take their talents and stay elsewhere and live elsewhere. At the same time they have this longing to come back here, and they look forward to that as a retirement.

They very much enjoy keeping in contact with what's going on here. They have a tendency to see the changes and be much more positive about the town, whereas the people who live here, I believe, because of their financial situation, because of self-esteem issues (a lot of the time), I think a lot of the people who live here feel trapped here.

Q. What are some of the down sides to living here?

A. Definitely for me and for what I see for a lot of people, it is the struggle to make a living, for number one. There's not a lot of stimulation. In other words, you've got to find your own, get your own group of friends or people to go with. Luckily we have La Crosse relatively close by, Dubuque. We're not that removed from places where you can find a little more stimulation. Then, luckily, there's the technological connection these days. You can communicate with people outside and feel a little more in tune.

But also, in a small town everyone likes to think they know your business. There's a lot of talk, there's a lot of—I don't know if it goes back to people feeling trapped here—(but) they don't want to see other people succeed. There's a lot of negativism. People aren't real good at encouraging other people; they're always looking on the dark side.

Change is difficult. You try to get involved in some community actions, express some concerns to city council members, or whatever, to try to get things improved or updated. That's difficult. People don't like to see change.

Q. What might turn things around? What could bring prosperity to town?

A. I'm an eternal optimist. I like to think that someday it is all going to come together here. I think it's going to have to come from within in a lot of ways. I don't know how you make people change. If people had a more positive attitude, a little more enthusiasm about things. How we get that I'm not real sure. How we draw the jobs, I don't know.

One of the things that has been real helpful has been the influx of professionals, people from the cities: some of our young people who have left and come back to try to find a niche here. I think they bring a lot of good ideas, a lot more enthusiasm. They're willing to get out and work on the beautification committee, willing to get out and help on LDC projects. They're more involved.

Part VI:

EPILOGUE

FATHER NORMAN WHITE

Now retired as Rural Life Director for the Dubuque Archdiocese, Father White has been a passionate and articulate defender of the family farm for the last decade. In a rural culture that values public silence in the matter of explosive issues, Father White has been unafraid to speak his mind. He is probably the best known small farm advocate in Iowa. This article consists of excerpts from an interview conducted in May 1995. I call it "Daniel in the Lion's Den."

Daniel in the Lion's Den

I became Rural Life Director in January of '83 on a part-time basis. I was pastor at Fayette and Hawkeye and continued on that way. And during that first year, 1993, I worked closely with the newly organized Land Stewardship Project out of St. Paul, working against soil erosion especially, setting up meetings in Iowa.

By December of '83, it was obvious that there was a need for more than legal advice and financial help, which we were providing. It was obvious that they needed spiritual help, too, and so I switched from working against soil erosion to concentrate on soul erosion. I got that terminology from Bishop Maurice Dingman when I first heard him talk to us Rural Life directors in Des Moines.

In the winter of early '84, in an attempt to help that soul erosion, we put on three retreats...Well, word got around the countryside that we were talking about the legal options for farmers as well as low input agriculture and that sort of thing. So a banker complained to an assistant bishop, who in turn told the archbishop and the archbishop in turn said to me, "By the way, a banker complained that you're bringing up legal things in these retreats."

I said, "Well, I'll talk to him, I'll call him. It's important that we understand that aspect."

I called him, he set up a meeting a few days later, and I said, "Who'll be there?"

He said, "Well, our loan officer, and our land bank director, because the land bank has an interest in a particular farm, and the extension director."

I asked who, and he told me. I said, "Oh? The regional director? Did you know he's the one who was quoted in *The Telegraph Herald* as referring to 'Father White and that save the family farm shit?' "

He said, "It won't be Daniel in the lion's den."

I said, "It will too, but I'll come. I need to know how things are from your aspect."

So I get there, and not only were those people present but their lawyer, a man whom I taught in high school. I was his principal, I taught him speech. Also present was the pastor of the place, a man whom I taught when he was in seminary.

Their main concern was that Chapter 11 was being used by a particular farmer who had a loan with them, and they felt he should not do that. "If they feel they cannot make any more, they should go to Chapter 7, which is outright bankruptcy."

I said, "That means you're the first mortgage, you'll get everything that's left, and Main Street, the businesses, won't get anything."

"Yeah, but they (the businesses) are not going to get more than even ten percent if they file Chapter 11, the way you're recommending."

Twice during our conversation they brought out the portfolio of this one particular family that they were concerned about, and that we'd been working closely with. The first time they did this I said, "You have no right to even show me that portfolio. I know them well, I've been on their farm. I don't know their situation, and you have no business revealing, professionally, where they stand." When they showed it the second time I repeated that: "It is not right, it is not fair. To me it's immoral, it's unprofessional."

We went on for a couple of hours, and I had a list of questions, but then they all went back to work. I never did report this back to the archbishop. He never did ask me about it. I reported it back to the auxiliary bishop who had received the call in the first place and told him who was there. And he said, "Oh, you mean it was five against two?" I said, "No, it was six against one. This pastor didn't say much, but when he did he was obviously being pressured to take the bank's side."

It was some months later that Prairiefire (a coalition of farm organizations) wanted to have a meeting in eastern Iowa to talk to farmers about their rights and what we should be doing and can be doing.

And the young fellow who was helping me visit farm homes said he would contact this particular parish to see if they could use the church hall. It was the same town where this bank meeting took place. The pastor immediately said, "Yes, you can use the hall." Before the day was over he called the farmer back and said, "No, you can't use the church hall."

But that's only one example of parishes that we have found very noncooperative. There's two pastors of a Protestant religion who wanted us there to do a retreat. So they arranged with one of the churches in town to have us there, but then, shortly afterwards they were informed by the leadership of that parish that the banker said, "That bunch is not meeting at our church." So they took us out to the fairgrounds.

There's another situation at a rather fundamentalist parish with a couple who worked with us a lot, trying to salvage some things. When they declared bankruptcy she was dismissed as a Sunday school teacher and he was dismissed as bus driver for their Sunday school, and then as they got into this thing further, they were dismissed from the parish, and they moved to another town.

The cruelty. It's part of this, "You have disgraced us by declaring bankruptcy." One of the problems I had out here was, why is it that business and industry can declare Chapter 7 and it's considered a wise move, good business, and when a farmer does it he's a bum?

Another woman who lost her farm, once they declared bankruptcy, did not receive the sign of peace from a member of her own choir for years. I don't know if she has yet.

I have never gotten very frank with the archbishop about the attitude of the Farm Bureau leadership in parishes because I'm sure they have gotten to him too. I'm positive of it.

***

I was to give two workshops for the Archdiocesan Council of Catholic Women, probably in 1986. One was in Waukon, and one was in the western part of the diocese. I went to the then president of the Dubuque county Farm Bureau. I went to his home and I said, "I am going to come out against your state leadership and national leadership in these workshops. I'm so sick and tired of Farm Bureau taking stances contrary to what the Catholic Church holds. Our bishops are talking about cooperation rather than competing." And he said to me, jabbing his finger, he said, "You're wrong! The Church is wrong! This is the United States! Here is the land of competition! Here we compete!" He said, "Furthermore, there's a first amendment to the constitution that separates church and state. You take care of church, I'll take care of agriculture!"

I said, "No way. It's not going to be that way. It's going to be a constant battle."

When the document "Strangers and Guests" was put together by the bishops of the Midwest in 1980, on land stewardship, land conservation, that sort of thing, the Farm Bureau fought that thing tooth and nail because of the things that were in there on conservation and the common good. They never use common good. It's MINE! The personal, individual rights thing.

The main architect of that document, John Hart from Carroll College in Montana, just told me recently they're still sore, and they're still doing all they can to work against what the Catholic Church stands for in conservation stewardship.

One of the state conservationists in our diocese told me that he knows of a parish where the pastor is not allowed to preach on conservation. There's another parish where the retired pastor said to me, "When I first came to this parish the leadership told me, 'Don't you ever let Father White preach in this pulpit.' "

***

I got my degree in U.S. History. I taught U.S. History, but I didn't know the rural story at all until I got this job, and people passed stuff to me. I probably had the job a few years before a NFO (National Farmers Organization) person gave me a copy of a report issued by the Committee of Economic Development in 1962. That document just really shook me. These were industrialists, and the closest thing to agriculture on that committee was someone who made ketchup. In there they said, "It's important that we get excess resources, people primarily, out of agriculture, off the land. We need to get rid of 2 million farmers." That was in '62. At that time we had 6.2 million farmers.

Towards the end of the document it said, "Now, of course, as more and more people leave the farm and come into the cities there will need to be a moderation of wages." Moderation which way? Flood the market with employees, then we can pay our price.

That committee on economic development apparently meets annually. It didn't meet again on agriculture until '74, twelve years later. They said, "We have succeeded in reducing the farm population by 2 million, we must need to decrease it even more. There are too many out there." And some time around there, too, there was a report put out by the young executives of the USDA talking about farm policies and what needs to be done. They said, "And of course if this was done it would result in the decrease in the number of farms, which we do not see as a bad thing."

And I'm convinced that the whole idea is that the fewer farmers you have the more coalition you can build, the more control you can have. And that's certainly the case now with the big farmers, the big land owners, they're not necessarily farmers themselves.

This was 1952. From 1942 to 1952 there was what's called the Steagall Amendment, calling for parity for farmers. Part of this was during the Second World War when there was a need for a lot of food, lot of markets, and during that ten-year period farmers were getting 110 percent of parity.

Parity is this: the price the farmer gets for his product is on a par with other elements of the economy, on a par with what he pays for things or on a par with what labor gets, or on a par with what manufacturing is making. The Steagall Amendment was not renewed when it expired in 1952. It was the intention of Congress at that time not to, because prices were for farmers. I'm sure that's the reason for it.

My dad became county treasurer in 1941. He remained county treasurer 18 years, and he told me that he could tell within a month after the Steagall Amendment expired that farmers were having more and more trouble paying their taxes because the price of their products started going down.

My brother, now on the farm, retired (he's eighty years old) considers himself a success because he convinced all of his sons not to farm for a living. Already in the sixties and seventies he said, "The government has a cheap food policy. It's not fair, we don't get a decent price for our product. We work, work, and work our tails off. It's not right because we're not getting the cost of production plus a profit."

The government's policy is a cheap food policy, and I compare it to the bread and circuses of Rome: keep the folks happy with cheap food. That's the bread, I'm not sure what the circuses are.

***

I feel that in the last ten years we have helped farmers go through pain. But at a hearing with our U.S. representative I said, "Unless you help us get better prices for the farmers, they're simply not going to make it." Then he said to me, "I think it's wonderful what you're doing to reach out to help the hurting farmers."

I said, "That's just a palliative, that's just to try to undo some of the damage."

So he talked on and on and finally I stopped him again. And he said, "It's great what you're doing."

I said, "I refuse to settle for being a pall bearer, helping the farmers bury their family farms. I just will not be a professional mourner, and only a professional mourner."

Well, I was that, I have been that. And we had quite a network of outreach to hurting farmers, and I don't think we've accomplished anything other than that.

***

I've given up, I have really given up on trying to help keep middle and small farmers on the land through any kind of political process, and we failed miserably. My main concern now is food security world wide, including our own urban people. Because when a few people get control of the whole food supply, from the oink in the hoghouse to the wow! in the supermarket, then you'll know that something long lasting has happened to all consumers.

ROBERT WOLF

Robert Wolf is executive director of Free River Press.

The Jeffersonian Ideal

According to *The Des Moines Register*, Iowa lost one-quarter of its farmers in the farm crisis of the 1980s and will lose another quarter in the 1990s. But the devastating Midwestern floods the summer of 1993 made it clear that it would take less than a decade to force that next quarter off the land. Today the small Iowa farmer knows that his years are numbered, and he knows that his and other Midwestern farm lands are being transferred into the hands of fewer and fewer owners.

About the end of World War II this country saw the triumph of efficiency as the standard by which to judge agricultural techniques. After the war tractors replaced plows, mules, and horses. Herbicides and pesticides were soon introduced. All this meant that farming was getting "scientific," along with the rest of efficiently run businesses.

Tractors and chemicals obviously increased costs, but farmers were persuaded to accept them because they decreased labor and increased the chances for greater profits through greater yields. When you think about it, it seems remarkable that organic farming, which farmers had practiced for millennia worldwide, should have been wiped out in a matter of decades. And yet it was, partly no doubt because of the appeal for anything "scientific," and partly because of potential profits. But now one of these elements of "scientific and advanced" farming — the expensive machinery — has become a major contributor to the small farmer's demise.

Even before the effect of machinery's high cost began to take its toll, farmers were persuaded to get big, to buy more land, and to plant "fence row to fence row." In the 1970s FmHA loans were easy to get. So farmers got big. They bought more land, added to their herds, maybe built a new milking barn or added to their farrowing operation. Then in the late seventies, nobody knows quite why, loans were sometimes called in or rewritten, sometimes underhandedly. A farmer might be asked to sign an agreement that put him out of business.

By the mid-1980s more than a handful of farm families were living through the winters without heat, and with very little food. Many watched their herds die of starvation. The strain cracked many. Divorce increased. And then came the suicides.

***

All this continues to lead our country away from its rural roots, into an ever stranger and more complex future, far from the agrarian vision of Thomas Jefferson, who wanted America filled with farmers, because he believed that they are "the most virtuous and independent citizens."

Rather than see Americans divided in employment between manufacture and agriculture, Jefferson wanted to leave manufacturing to the Europeans, for the United States, he thought, could purchase needed goods from Europe in exchange for American food surpluses. One of the biggest arguments in favor of such an arrangement, he argued, was the physical and moral superiority "of the agricultural, over the manufacturing, man."

To John Jay he wrote: "We have now lands enough to employ an infinite number of people in their cultivation. Cultivators of the earth are the most valuable citizens. They are the most vigorous, & they are tied to their country & wedded to it's (sic) liberty & interests by the most lasting bonds. As long as they can find employment in this line I would not convert them into mariners, artisans or anything else."

But on the day Americans become too numerous for the land, then, Jefferson thought, "I should then perhaps wish to turn them to the sea in preference to manufacture, because comparing the characters of the two classes I find the former the most valuable citizens. I consider the class of artificers of a country as the panders of vice & the instruments by which the liberties of a country are generally overturned."

By "artificers" he means the makers of goods, artisans and manufacturers, those who employ themselves alone and those who employ hundreds. What is decisive for Jefferson is that manufacture breeds a demand for luxuries, and is opposed to frugality, a civic virtue. He had in mind the examples of the ancient world, particularly Rome, where a tough and free people acquired a wealth and luxury which corrupted them to the point where they abandoned their liberties for a dictatorship. Even in the early days of the republic, Jefferson considered "the extravagance which has seized them (Americans) as a more baneful evil than toryism was during the war." If Jefferson thought Americans were corrupted then by luxuries, what would he say to us today?

***

The framers of our constitution understood the intimate connection between economics and politics, between money and political power. "(Alexander) Hamilton and his school," historian Charles Beard wrote, "deliberately sought to attach powerful interests to the Federal Government. Jefferson clung tenaciously to the proposition that freehold agriculture bore a vital relation to the independence of spirit essential to popular rule." Hence Jefferson's passionate desire to see America's lands filled with freehold farmers.

In 1821, not many years after Jefferson's presidency, American statesman Daniel Webster wrote: "It seems to me to be plain that, in the absence of military force, political power naturally and necessarily goes into the hands which hold the property." The early English settlers of New England, he wrote, "were themselves. . . nearly on a general level in respect to property. Their situation demanded a parcelling out and division of the lands, and it may be fairly said that this necessary act *fixed the future and form of their government.* The character of their political institutions was determined by the fundamental laws respecting property. . . . The consequence of all these causes has been a great subdivision of the soil and a great equality of condition; the true basis, most certainly, of popular government."

Webster, then, agreed with Jefferson that popular government rested upon the wide distribution of land among its citizens. Jefferson went further, wanting an agriculturally based economy for the country, because farmers were the best of all classes to uphold their liberty, first by their independence, and second by their lack of corruption. But the powerful and emerging mercantile, banking, and manufacturing interests in the developing country would eventually subvert that dream. Speaking on behalf of those interests, Alexander Hamilton wrote: "The prosperity of commerce is now perceived and acknowledged by all enlightened statesmen to be the most useful as well as the most productive source of national wealth . . ." By the 1920s commercial and financial interests had triumphed to the point where Calvin Coolidge could proclaim that "the business of America is business."

***

When we examine traditional civilizations, we find that one thinker after another warns us of the perils of commerce and finance. The argument, though, is from a different point of view than that of Jefferson, who is himself echoing the fears of Roman stoics. The stoics saw that wealth and luxury had corrupted the Roman people, but for Plato and others the argument against business revolved around its ability to corrupt the arts. For the Greeks and other traditional peoples, art was not confined to painting, sculpture, music, literature, and dance. The word 'art' itself is our clue to that, deriving as it does from the Latin word 'ars,' meaning skill, trade, or profession, as well as 'art' in our restricted sense. Thus in traditional societies anyone who made a thing was an artist. So were those who nurtured, such as physicians and farmers.

Underlying the very foundations of traditional societies was the knowledge that to lead a fully human existence a person must have an art that he follows all his life. The distinction between work and labor lies in the fact that work is imbued with art, shaped by it, and labor lacks art. Strip a person's livelihood of art, and you strip him of his humanity. A person stripped of his humanity eventually turns to violence, and much of the anger in this country comes from people working jobs that are better suited to robots than to human beings. As for farmers forced off the land, most are obliged to trade a complex art with multiple activities and skills, for low-skilled labor.

***

To understand how fully the deck is stacked against farmers you must understand that with few exceptions the only farmers who stand a chance

128

of crawling out from under debt are those who can somehow market their own products directly to consumers. Otherwise they are locked into a price determined primarily by the five major international grain corporations, two of which are U.S. based. These multi-national corporations are the purveyors of wheat, corn, soybeans, rice, and other grains to governments around the world. Indirectly these company determine, here and abroad, the price of livestock and poultry, as well as bread, cereals, pasta, and other grain based produce. It is these companies, not the U.S. government, which sells U.S. wheat to Russia, Korea, and elsewhere.

In years when the sales of the multi-national grain corporations to foreign governments are relatively low, their influence is lessened, while that of the futures markets in Chicago, Minneapolis, and Kansas City is increased. But the major grain corporations have independent brokers buying and selling futures contracts for them at these markets. Considering the volume at which they buy and sell, their influence is considerable.

The prices on grain, pork, beef, and other commodities can vary widely within a day, affected by weather, scarcity, foreign sales and other factors. The middlemen, speculators, never actually see what they are buying or selling, and most fail to make a profit, but those who succeed can make a fortune. Such middlemen are unnecessary, and are symptomatic of a society whose driving force is avarice. As R.H. Trawney wrote in *Religion and the Rise of Capitalism*, medieval social theory condemned "the speculator or the middleman, who snatches private gain by the exploitation of public necessities."

Those farmers who are willing to play the very involved game of puts and calls on the commodities markets may protect themselves from loss. But the majority of farmers, nine out of ten, do not speculate on the market, and do not want to. It is not in their nature. Yet the politicians, the bureaucrats in the U.S. Department of Agriculture, and the bankers are expecting the farmer to become a "good manager," which means they expect him not only to use a computer to record his yields, profits, and losses, but to utilize the latest developments in biotechnology, and to operate successfully in the futures markets. But the farmer is a special kind of artist, and to ask him to abandon his art and take up someone else's is to expect him to violate his nature.

This brings us to the very heart of this "civilization's" malaise: the denigration and abandonment of vocation, which is intimately connected to the idea of art. In traditional civilizations, all people had a vocation. A vocation is a calling to this or that kind of work, and this calling is determined by our aptitude, which directs our love. This is to say that we love what we do well or what we are called to do. But few remember the idea of vocation, or if they remember it, dismiss it, for we are a pragmatic people, and as pragmatists we can see no difference between work and labor.

Today the values of the commercial class are those that drive this society and its institutions. One outcome is that today, as in Plato's time, commerce has infected all the arts. Artists of various kinds, physicians, surgeons, and lawyers among them, confuse the art of making money with their own special arts. The small farmer has resisted, asking only for a fair price and the opportunity to continue farming.

But the pragmatist has no use for the small farmer, who is inefficient. He is inefficient because he is not a "good manager." And being inefficient, he is undesirable. As former Secretary of Agriculture Earl Butz has said repeatedly, "There are too many farmers." But what this society has yet to learn is that efficiency is a totally inappropriate standard by which to judge human beings and their work, though an appropriate one for robots.

To work backward, the farm crisis can be seen as the final clash between the urban forces of commerce and banking on the one hand, and agrarian, democratic interests on the other. The issue of the contest is not much in doubt, and when the farmer and his way of life pass on, the fiber of American democracy passes with him.

***

There is a beautiful book recently published, a forty year record of farm families in Jo Daviess County, Illinois. In this book, *Neighbors*, one of the farmers says. "...I love this land, all right. To me the land is my being. It's all I've got. It's my existence. I feel like I'm just a part of it. When you read in the Bible where it says God gave you this land to till it, to take care of it, to prosper, that's what it means to me. It's my duty to do this. I don't consider it a job exactly. It's a duty. A responsibility. That gives me happiness and satisfaction and a reason for being here."

How many of us can say that we have a responsibility to do our work, beyond the responsibility to provide food and shelter for our families? For the vast majority of us, our work means nothing more than a paycheck. We have not found what the Buddhists call "right livelihood." We have not found our vocation, so do not know what it is we are supposed to do, have not found responsibility, and consequently remain irresponsible. But a society composed of people without duty and responsibility has no human-centered course or direction. Without duty we are alienated, and that accounts, in part, for why so many of us are angry, why there is so much violence.

It is fitting to close with a passage from Thomas Jefferson, a passage from one of his letters to James Madison that has proved prophetic: "I think our governments will remain virtuous for many centuries; as long as they are chiefly agricultural; and this will be as long as there shall be vacant lands in any part of America. When they get piled upon one another in large cities, as in Europe, they will become corrupt as in Europe, and go to eating one another as they do there."

Developing Regional Rural Economies

by Robert Wolf

The following is a six-part radio commentary on the need for rural Americans to develop self-sufficient regional economies, written for broadcast over KUNI in Cedar Falls, Iowa, a National Public Radio affiliate. The commentary won the Society of Professional Journalist's Sigma Delta Chi Award for best radio editorial of 1994.

When I moved to rural Iowa, almost three years ago, I did not know the troubles it faced. I had heard of rural flight, but as an urban dweller, not facing the daily reality of rural life, I ignored the rural crisis.

I moved here, to northeast Iowa, because I wanted to live in beauty and relative solitude, because I thought it might be possible to have a culturally rich life in rural America. I know now that I was overly optimistic and naive. I had, in fact, very little idea of what it would mean to live on an isolated farm ten miles from either of the nearest towns, trying to earn a living as a writer and publisher.

When I moved here I believed what possibly many others believe: that rural America is a place where people still gather in community, sure in themselves and their friends. I believed the land and water were pure and uncontaminated, even though I had read and heard otherwise. I believed that the best of modern technology had been absorbed, the worst rejected. I believed all these things because I did not live in rural America.

Perhaps I had been affected by the television commercials which try to sell products by identifying them with farms and country towns. I believe that many of us still associate rural America with what is uncontaminated and cleanest in ourselves. It is a myth which helps sustain us. Like the ever-shrinking wilderness, we must have it, at least in our fantasies, a land or town where it is still possible to escape from an ever-more frantic and directionless society.

But that, as I said, turns out to have been extremely optimistic and naive. The fact is that rural America is dying.

There is little energy and self-confidence here. And little work. The farmers are leaving their lands for low-skilled jobs in the cities. What few jobs small towns do offer pay mostly minimum wage. The young people, those who can, leave as soon as the high school diploma is in their hands.

What can we do?

***

I live in the Third World, in Iowa, not far from the Mississippi River. Oh yes, Iowa is part of the Third World, and so is most of rural America. If you need convincing, just look at what third world countries do, then look at rural America.

Typically a third world country has natural resources and human labor that it's willing to sell for a pittance, resources and labor that developed countries want, especially at bargain prices.

Does that fit rural America? You bet. Rural America exports its produce and livestock, and in exchange receives a pittance. That is, the family farmer does. The profits from the small farmer's produce, stock, and hard work go to someone else, usually out of state. On the other hand, the corporate farmer makes good money because he's farming in volume. But the corporate farmer, more than likely, does not live in rural America, but in some large metropolitan center like Chicago or Dallas. Thus the profits made from family and corporate farms flow from rural to urban America.

The condition of the third world country worsens as its resources are gobbled up and its workers and farmers become more and more destitute. We see that happening here in Iowa. Corn, Iowa's biggest crop, because it is grown year after year, takes an enormous toll on one of Iowa's greatest natural resources, its soil. But federal subsidies for corn growers encourages this loss. And, of course, Iowa farmers, thanks to the present agricultural system, remain poor and continue leaving the land in a steady stream.

This situation occurs in third world countries when the industry and agricultural methods of developed countries—the colonizers—disrupt the traditional way of life in the colonies. It lures peasants from their land and villages for jobs in factories, mines, and deforestation crews.

Likewise, rural Americans continue to leave the countryside for opportunity elsewhere. Rural America's most valuable export, more important than its grain and livestock, is its high school and college graduates. They can't afford to stay.

The colonizer's economy takes away the native's self-sufficiency in a local economy and replaces it with dependence on the colonizer's economy. Control of their own lives is no longer in the hands of the locals. That's Iowa's situation, and the situation of every other rural area in this nation, where local and regional economies have been destroyed, first under the development the national economy, later under pressure from an ever-growing international economy.

Meanwhile no one in Washington seems particularly concerned about the state of the third world within its own borders.

***

From the urbanite's point of view there probably is no reason to keep rural America alive. Most urbanites don't know where their food comes from, and don't much care. It makes no difference to them whether their food is grown on a family farm or corporate farm. Big or small is irrelevant to the final product, which should be tasty, clean, and brightly colored, if not smartly packaged.

I am afraid that our federal officials and bureaucrats share this sentiment about our food, its source, and the state of rural economies. At least I have not heard of any rural policy positions or programs emanating from the White House or Capitol Hill.

When President Clinton was first elected I did read or hear something about the administration's concern for building a rural development program, and now two years later, this spring, he convened a rural development conference in Iowa. But it was a symbolic gesture, and like much else the president has done, it seemed half-hearted, without passion or commitment.

About a year ago I called Senator Harkin's office, and asked his top aide if he could tell me which think tanks in this country were developing rural policy. He mentioned The Center for Rural Affairs in Wald Hill, Nebraska, but I knew about that. Nothing else came to his mind. He said he would research it and call me back. That was over a year ago and he has yet to make that phone call.

I now think that Washington's indifference is a blessing. When President Reagan began dismantling federal programs, in the belief that problems were better handled on state and local levels, I was angry. But now I think he was right. National programs cannot be flexible enough to adjust to local conditions. More important, a centrally directed program will not develop what needs to be developed: economic self-sufficiency and local initiative.

No one is going to solve our problems for us. We have only our brains to rely on, and if they are stuffed with inadequate ideas we're going to pay a heavy price. No one from the outside is going to give us a wonderful future. No one from New York or Los Angeles is going to hand us a three billion dollar check.

We create our own future. Either we decide what it is we want, and go after it, or someone else will decide it for us. If we are actively going to create our future, instead of waiting for it passively to happen, we must first decide the kind of future we want. Which means we must work cooperatively. We must think together.

***

So long as Iowans and other rural residents believe that they can rebuild their economies and spirits within the existing economic system, their situation will worsen.

When most rural Americans think of improving their local economies, they usually think of either attracting more tourists or of recruiting factories. We have all heard of desperate towns across America giving tax incentives and outright cash to companies that will locate within their borders. And time and again we have heard of these same companies, having gotten a free ride, pulling out for another desperate town or country where costs are even lower. Rural Americans would do better to create their own businesses.

But this will not happen until rural America has banks committed to local development. Perhaps you have that kind of bank in your town, but where I live people complain that the only ones who get loans are those who don't need them.

That sort of conservatism is anathema to healthy commerce. Rural America needs banks like the South Shore Bank of Chicago, a black-owned bank committed to the economic development of Chicago's black South Shore district. That bank has developed black businesses, and rebuilt South Shore's prosperity. Now it is working for the development of a portion of rural Arkansas.

But some have despaired of the present banking system altogether, including one rural Vermont town that has decided to secede from the U.S.

banking system, and has developed its own scrip. Because of disenchant-
ment with so many institutions, I suspect that in years to come we will hear
more about the need for rural areas to unhitch themselves from the federal
reserve system and build their own banks and issue their own currencies.
What does seem clear is that so long as Iowa and other rural areas
remain Third World countries, depending on the crumbs from the colonizer's
economy for their maintenance, so long as the colonizers run the factories,
farms, and banks, so long will rural America be poor.

***

     I began thinking about rural economic
development when I first heard Warren Rudman's claim that if the United
States does not drastically reduce its national deficit that someday it will
become the world's largest banana republic.
Whether or not the deficit will trigger collapse, other factors force rural Americans to think about constructing arks, self-sufficient economic
and social entities that can survive the hard times that are upon us.
My own town, Lansing, could not possibly be self-sufficient, but what
size area could be? For some reason, perhaps because of the shared land-
scape of hills and winding valleys and their farm economies, I began to
think of northeast Iowa, southeast Minnesota, and southwest Wisconsin. I
began to wonder whether this area could be self-sufficient.
Someone told me that it has a name, the Driftless Bioregion, so-called
because the glaciers did not drift over it. That same person said that northwest Illinois, including Galena, was a part of it.
I learned that people around the country were thinking of bioregions as
determinants of future economic and cultural units, not in terms of the nation or of states. The important point when developing an ark is to think in
terms of shared values and habits. A bioregion can provide this.
The Driftless Bioregion unifies us by virtue of its topography, which in
turn defines agricultural practice. And that practice defines our opportuni-
ties and limitations. We are bound together in many ways, some not always obvious.
Most of the counties of this bioregion, for example, are poor, about the
poorest in their respective states. And that's because of our topography,
which means our farms are not as rich as flatland farms.
But, with the application of imagination and courage, this poor region
could be transformed into a land of wealth.
Already imaginative and energetic people from Minneapolis and St.

Paul are moving into southeast Minnesota and setting up businesses; people from Madison and Chicago have moved into southwest Wisconsin. Fewer have ventured into northeast Iowa, because of its greater distance from the major cities. But it will happen, I'm sure, it's just a matter of time.

***

As I've said, a regional economy can provide an ark, a social and economic unit that can enable us to weather these hard times, and those ahead. A self-sufficient regional economy is not a Third World economy, nor a region of the colonized.

A regional economy cannot be built directly, but in steps, and indirectly.

In the case of the Driftless Bioregion, encompassing southeast Minnesota, northeast Iowa, southwest Wisconsin, and northwest Illinois, the first intermediate step is to begin envisioning a Regional City for each of these areas.

A regional City is another name for what has been called The Social City. The Regional City, as it is usually envisioned, is an aggregate of cities, not of towns. The point of the Social or Regional City is to maintain a greenbelt between individual cities to prevent the development of one mass megalopolis.

There are only three cities within The Driftless Bioregion with populations of over 10,000 persons, so the Regional Cities we might build are radically different from what is usually envisioned. But for both kinds, cooperation between towns or cities is imperative to its functioning. If one town or city developed a technical college or a major hospital, others would refrain from duplicating it. The pie, after all, is only so big.

Major economic and cultural domains, such as tourism, industry, and transportation, would be addressed in common planning sessions, to develop overall strategy.

In 1993 Joseph Lempke, studio professor of architecture at the Illinois Institute of Technology, sent a proposal to ten or so small towns of northeast Iowa, stating that for $500 per town the students of his planning class would undertake the task of drawing up a blueprint for transforming northeast Iowa into a Regional City.

The price was modest, and the insight that we might have gained could have been enormous. But the towns turned down the project.

One of the biggest problems in small towns is their inability to work cooperatively. Towns see each other as rivals, or potential rivals. And to complicate matters, most small towns are divided into factions.

Perhaps the situation will not improve, perhaps it will worsen. But the vision of a bioregional economy connected by Regional Cities remains a possibility, and a vision that is loved, be it good or evil, can be willed, and being willed, can be actualized.

FREE RIVER PRESS
Folk Literature Series

Robert Wolf, ed. **Passing Thru.** $4.95
El Gilbert. **Lion's Share.** $4.95
Josef Goller. **From within Walls.** $4.95
Diana Schooler. **Lemme Tell You where I Used to Live.** $4.95
Rebel Yell. **Hitchhiker's Dream.** $4.95
Robert Wolf, ed. **Voices from the Land.** $5.95
Steve Abatte, **Pawns.** $6.50
Clara Leppert, **Simple Times.** $5.95
Robert Wolf, ed. **More Voices from the Land.** $5.95
Robert Wolf, ed. **Independence, Iowa.** $6.95
Robert Wolf, ed. **Clermont, Iowa.** $6.50
Robert Wolf, ed. **Franklin-Gateway.** $6.50